TANGYE

TANGYE

David Power

David Power

The Book Guild Ltd
Sussex, England

The Book Guild Ltd.
25 High Street,
Lewes, Sussex

First published 2000
© David Power 2000

Set in Times
Typesetting by
SetSystems Ltd, Saffron Walden, Essex

Printed in Great Britain by
Bookcraft (Bath) Ltd, Avon

A catalogue record for this book is
available from the British Library

ISBN 1 85776 478 1

To Barbara, whose loyalty made the writing of this book very enjoyable.

ACKNOWLEDGEMENT

This book is a dual biography and it is with heartfelt thanks to Jean Nicol Tangye's sister, Barbara, that I dedicate it to her.

The writer of such a work knows, only too well, that the subject matter depends so much on the willingness and the frankness of those who contribute in the researching stage. The writing of *Tangye* was supported by many of Derek and Jeannie's friends and associates and I am eternally grateful for their participation and goodwill. Each and every one has subscribed to the Tangye legend.

I would also like to acknowledge the very significant roles played by: Harrow College, Copthorne Preparatory School and the Savoy Hotel.

PREFACE

It is with immense pride and honour that I have been asked to write the Preface for a book about one of my illustrious predecessors in the Savoy Group Press Office, Jean Nicol Tangye.

To me, Jean was the embodiment of the Savoy: stylish and glamorous, and, above all, a truly passionate individual. She represented a nostalgic bygone era and yet that same tradition and subtle continuity remain at the hotel today. Working in the Press Office today is not as glamorous in many ways as it was in Jean's day but it is equally alluring and magical. The signed photographs of hundreds of celebrities from Marilyn Monroe to Judy Garland and Elizabeth Taylor surround us in our Press Office, like they did in Jean's day, and are testimony to the timeless appeal of the hotel.

Reading David Power's marvellous tribute to Jean Nicol Tangye is a powerful reminder of the privileged and exciting position I fortunately find myself in. Although I never met Jean I feel I know her intimately: her spirit lives on and her passion for the Savoy never dies. As Jean herself said: 'I grew to love it with a love that was as strong as it was unreasonable; a love that disturbed my dreams as well as my days until I thought and spoke of nothing else.'

Julia Record
Director of Communications, The Savoy Group.

FOREWORD

I first became aware of Jean Nicol Tangye when I started work as a press office assistant in room 205 at the Savoy Hotel. Shortly after my arrival, in December 1989, it was decided to hold a reunion lunch for all past press officers and on the designated day a crowd of chattering ladies entered the office – they were followed closely by an elderly gentleman who leaned on a walking stick.

The quiet man was introduced to me as Derek Tangye and he had been invited to the luncheon to represent perhaps the most famous Savoy group press officer of them all, his wife Jean – who had died a few years earlier. I was fortunate to sit next to him at the dining table and discovered an instant rapport. He was charming, erudite and had an ability to make you feel that, for the moment, you were the most important person in the world. The meeting ended with an invitation to visit him in Minack but, sadly, I never took up his offer.

Over the years that followed I was constantly contacted by readers of Jean's book *Meet Me at the Savoy*, who wanted to visit the room she had made famous while working there in the 1940s – room 205. Her devotees came to stay from far corners of the world and, in recent times, it has been with great pride that I have been able to show them her framed picture that now hangs on the 'stars wall' that she started and made famous in her day.

After meeting Derek Tangye I began to read, in the *Minack Chronicles*, of the lifestyle he and Jeannie shared on their remote Cornish clifftop, and through the books I felt I had come to know something of Jean's personality and I discovered the spark that had made her such a popular figure at the Savoy Hotel.

Although I met Derek several times in the years that followed, I was not able to visit the cottage at Minack until after his death in 1996; and when I did I experienced the spirit that remains in the sanctuary that will always nestle in that beautiful corner of England.

That precious picture of Derek and Jeannie Tangye will remain forever on the wall of the press office of The Savoy to celebrate a very remarkable couple.

Pam Carter
PR Manager
The Savoy Group
October 1999

INTRODUCTION

As individualists, Derek and Jeannie Tangye stood alone, holding hands, within a crowd that was unable to perceive the naive enthusiasm that inspired them to journey on an unknown road to Minack – an odyssey that led them from the rapid tearing of the leaves of a busy social calendar to an easing in life's swift pace.

They were enchanted by the dream of a place that was unreal to others, where a romantic fantasy germinated and flowered within a perception that was theirs alone – its rhythm of life gentle and harmonious. It was in contrast to the patterns of thought of a busy city that demanded a symmetry of straight lines and square edges.

High on an isolated plateau, above the craggy coastline of south-west Cornwall, where the age-worn granite cairn of Carne Barges looked out over Mount's Bay, they perceived their kismet in a stone cottage that had evolved of distant time – and in its infinite existence it still dwells within a heavenly peace.

Time, unlike music, has no coda. Music can be played at will, reviving emotion, while time contrives to slip quietly away. At Minack, there remains a spring of clear water in the occasion of that time, and through the *Minack Chronicles* life has become constant – for as long as that water shall flow.

1

By the time the month of March had arrived in 1934, London was more than ready to bid farewell to a cold insensitive winter. Ashen clouds still hovered over the West End as pedestrians trod the pavements, heads down to the wind, walking in each other's footsteps. Men were huddled in heavy overcoats, the more affluent with curly black wool astrakhan collars and silk scarves. For some, a contemporary black homburg hat was placed firmly on the head. Women with a sense of fashion wore broad fur collars on coats that hugged the waistline. Many had long slim-fitting skirts that showed just a little of a calf that was shaped by an elegant high-heeled shoe.

Class and social identity in 1930s London was very much about hats as a mode of division. Tradesmen preferred to don a cloth cap. The young male admirer of the Chicago gangster in Hollywood movies wore a trilby, the front brim pulled down over the eyes. Doormen and commissionaires wore a smart military-type hat with a decorated peak. The bowler hat was symbolic of an achieved position of respect and was, therefore, worn by some of the men in a rather pretentious manner.

Derek Tangye was a humble clerk working at Unilever House in New Bridge Street. He wore a bowler hat as an integral part of his city businessman's suit, for which he was unqualified. He walked with intent in his stride in the image of a young man, just turned 22 years of age, who steered a privileged career ahead of him – a career that would seem to promise an eventual seat in a boardroom. With a folded umbrella hooked over his left forearm he imparted the bearing of a young subaltern in civilian clothes. But his appearance gave false witness to the clear and positive attitude that his body language suggested, as he jostled his way among the walkers of Ludgate Circus.

His destination was a bleak building that was opened for questionable business behind the façade of an unkempt shopfront. It had an empty plateglass window space that displayed many rectangular charts of bald heads which were marked with lines that crossed each other to form boxed compartments of irregular shapes. Each section was impressed with words that, to a phrenologist, would reveal the talents and personality traits of any curious client who cared to step inside – no appointment was necessary.

Derek Tangye's outward appearance was a contradiction of the insecurity he felt in himself. He had witnessed the achievements of his two older brothers – Nigel as an accomplished flyer and Colin an accountant of merit. His mother and father, in their need to understand him and to give direction, had always been there for him with unquestioning support. Now he was feeling unfulfilled and could see no obvious future for himself. For quite some time he had aspired to a career in journalism but was lately deterred by the insidious manner in which many dehumanising stories were gathered by the renowned press of Fleet Street.

His love of music was aesthetically highbrow. Since childhood, both literature and art had played a critical role in his life and he had later been privileged with an opportunity to be educated at Harrow – but he had failed every examination he sat. As a scholar he was pedantic. He relished, far more, those moments he was able to sit quietly alone with introspective thoughts – and it became alluring to him that by simply seeking to know himself better, he might be privileged to have a tiny peep through the curtain that obscured his future.

As he settled, uncomfortably ill-at-ease in an upright wooden chair, he felt the ends of the phrenologist's fingers move and momentarily pause as they searched his scalp. He waited in eager anticipation of an utterance that would miraculously change his life; for without it he feared he would be condemned to a life that could only, at its best,

2

offer him the dreary status of a company representative – selling soap.

'You must not *barter!*' the phrenologist's voice insisted intuitively, after a furious and final burst of stroking Derek's head bumps.

Derek Tangye became instantly convinced that an oracle had addressed him, and he departed from the consulting room and walked Ludgate Circus with two inches added to every stride that took him back to Unilever House. His mind was clear now and he was about to make his very first independent decision in self-determination.

2

The foundation of a national monument in London seemed appropriate in the immediate anticipation of the birth of Derek Alan Trevithick Tangye. The Queen Victoria Memorial reflected the staid sobriety of the nation's longest-serving monarch and was symbolic of two generations of the Tangye name who had served her faithfully.

On Thursday 29 February 1912 (Leap Year's Day), Sophie Elizabeth Frieda Tangye – sometimes affectionately known to her husband Richard as "Frieda" – gave birth to her third son. It was a very normal birth to a middle-class well-to-do family and the event took place in an upstairs front bedroom of an Edwardian house at 40 Bramham Gardens in Earls Court, London. The dwelling place was a tall building and the nursery, where six-year-old Colin and three-year-old Nigel were suitably confined for such an occasion, was tucked conveniently away in the upper reaches on the fifth floor.

When the baby drew its first breath, its shrill cries were instantly carried upstairs, to the nanny's ears. The young woman was, at that moment, quite unaware of the gender of what was to be her new charge. However, she secretly hoped she would be making a little girl's pretty dress for the future, instead of a third sailor-boy suit.

1912 was a notable year to be born, for it was the time when Captain Scott had struggled heroically to reach the South Pole. The first non-stop aeroplane had flown from Paris to London. The *Titanic* tragically sank with heavy loss of life. On the first day of March (one day after the birth) suffragettes embarked on a campaign of shop window smashing in London in their fight for women's rights; Sophie Tangye admired the determination of these women but

4

regretted their public disorder. She was a woman of strong mind herself and was to become a role model for all three of her sons as they grew up. Spirited, she would imbue them with a strength of character that was infectious of her own and, as individuals, show them how to stand alone in a world that she knew would demand much of them.

Richard Trevithick Gilberstone Tangye was known fondly to his wife as "Gibby"; an abbreviation of his third given name. He was much respected in his dedication in upholding the law, as a barrister, and he was an exemplary husband and father. Although his household was considered, at that time, to be more humble than would have been thought for such a venerated member of the legal profession, it retained a cook, a parlourmaid, a chambermaid and a chauffeur, as well as a nanny.

In what was a reforming society, such living standards were to change; and the more aristocratic of professions would have to adapt their lifestyles accordingly. However, the Tangye boys were to be forever grateful for those initial circumstances that were provided by their father. Such an over-privileged early impression of life was inclined to implant its own attitude in a young mind, and when, in later life, they became more humbled through circumstance and occasion, they would be judged by that very attitude: something with which Colin and Nigel would have little difficulty – but in Derek it became a trait that followed him around like a mangy dog.

From the early nursery days, the affection that was shown to Derek and his two brothers by their father was indeed warm, but almost without emotion and they instinctively knew it was something they had to accept. Each morning he visited them in the nursery before leaving for the Law Courts. He had very little physical contact with any of his sons and often his only communication would be as a soft playful bear-like growl. He was not an emotionally demonstrative man. If he showed anger in the courtroom then it was a bit of professional "theatre" and it took a concerted effort on his part. However, Derek always found his

5

mother's presence an inspiration to him. What his father lacked in communication, his mother compensated for with a comforting manner and a ready smile of compassion and understanding.

In the years ahead, whenever Derek thoughtfully wandered back through the store-cupboard of his memories, those of his childhood made him feel sheltered in the security of their happiness. His recollections of 40 Bramham Gardens were dominated by its high-ceilinged drawing room. There were heavy curtains and thick plush carpets that graced the windows and the floors, and these had boastfully been purchased from Harrods. In his mind's eye he saw the tall, elegant glazed doors that were always opened on warm evenings, leading onto a balcony that gave a view of the neat green lawns of the railed park-like communal gardens below, shaded by tall beech and elm trees.

As a child it was strangely comforting to have in his nostrils the aroma of his father's Abdulla cigarette – it somehow wafted in an atmosphere that was soothing, and sometimes there lingered from the opened door of the study a deep rich fragrance from the ornate bowl of a briar pipe.

An imposing Beckstein grand piano dwelled in one corner of the drawing room, protected from the sunlight by curtains that were caringly drawn across the window beside it. Richard Tangye was a man of his time and, truly with Victorian values, he was fascinated by gadgets. His love of classical music had influenced him to purchase, at great cost, a pre-programmed pneumatically operated mechanical instrument that fitted neatly over the piano keyboard; and it played with the virtuosity of a fine concert hall performer. Yet another device, which was also somehow ahead of its time, magically brought the most excellent performances of many fine musicians and orchestras into the comfort of the living room each Sunday evening. Such home concerts were made possible through a network of private cable lines that were distributed from the nearby Albert Hall and, through subscription, one was directed into the Edwardian house at

40 Bramham Gardens. After tea the table was hurriedly cleared. The room was then prepared with much enthusiasm and excitement and, as the concert started, the family sat in comfortable armchairs and listened through headphones as if they were ensconced in front row seats watching the conductor as he waved his baton. Classical music was to remain an emotional haven throughout Derek's life.

Sunday morning, however, was regarded in a sense that was to indicate Sophie Tangye's need of spiritual development. She was fulfilled by the teachings of the Christian Scientist Church – but her husband did not share her commitment in faith and constantly excused himself as a non-practising Christian. Once every two weeks she walked with her three young sons, dressed in their "Sunday best" suits, to attend the service that was held at the Christian Scientist Church at Queen's Gate, just half a mile from Bramham Gardens. She was proud of her children's manners and the way they clearly presented themselves when spoken to by fellow worshippers – especially within earshot of the preacher. She felt the responsibility of her children's spiritual well-being was of her own behest. But her mind progressed in a different direction when she became aware of a spiritual conflict that smouldered in an unplumbed cavern within her soul and, concerned that her children should continue to relate to the words of her own expression, she became an orthodox Protestant and from then on, the lesson was often to be read at home to retain a measure of control over what would impress their young minds.

Just as it was the complexity of figures that bewitched and charmed Colin's mind as he grew up, so it was the expressive capacity of selected words as the building blocks in storytelling that fascinated both Nigel and Derek; for such was the composition of the exciting adventure fiction of their boyhood escapist years. The world beyond the narrative became a pipe-dream of the future for them – a parable of their own destiny. In the grown-up world, Nigel would become an accomplished writer long before Derek.

7

Their father's library was situated immediately above the kitchen in the house at Bramham Gardens and, when they became old enough, the three boys were allowed to browse among the vast collection of books that embraced almost every subject of merit for a thinking person. Sophie Tangye often gathered her sons around her there and, as they became engrossed in the story she read them, they would all smell the delight of the roastings that wafted from the kitchen below.

Gladys Garland became the children's nanny. She was young, slim and softly spoken – an improvement on her predecessor. As far as her charges were concerned, she was much more agreeable because she did not persist in the embarrassing habit of kissing them. And it was, indeed, much credit to her expertise that when Nigel became ill with chickenpox, both Derek and Colin remained uninfected by the disease. But it was an anomaly that an ailing youngster should receive more than an ample share of attention from both of the parents, and the nanny also – thus creating a jealous sense of rivalry within the nursery.

3

The contentment that Derek Tangye felt of his early child-hood days became an instrument of recall as he went through his life. In his memory such satisfaction pre-empted the period where shadows often prevailed over the intangible dreams of youth – when dreams were sometimes interpreted as a prediction of what is to come. As an adult, he leaned heavily on such past associations as the combination of a favourite wine and Chopin's Fantasy in F Minor, Op. 49. This encouraged him to ease back in his chair and to close his eyes. It took no effort for the piano recital he was hearing to become the result of the pneumatic device that once sprawled over the keys of the Bechstein grand piano in the drawing room of the Edwardian house. And, in his mind's eye, he could see the French windows opened wide, and he could feel a temperate evening air that was aromatic with the smell of new-mown grass.

He was to see again, through the safety bars in the window of the nursery that towered five storeys above the quiet street, a two-wheeled horse-drawn cart, as the milk-man ladled some of the contents of a galvanised churn into a large pewter measure, to be transferred to a kitchen container at the tradesmen's entrance to the house; his blinkered horse constantly munched in a nosebag of oats. Later in the day came the muffin man who balanced a large flat tray on his head with the ease of practice. With his free hand he rang a bell, like a schoolma'am, and with a voice like that of a town crier he announced his arrival. But most mysterious of all to a child of that era was the lamplighter. Appearing at dusk and again at dawn this silent man, in a cloth peaked cap, rode a bicycle slowly whilst balancing a long pole on his shoulder. He hooked a small metal arm at the top of each lamp-post and a gas mantle popped into a warm light. He left Bramham Gardens at the far end of the road – and when he was gone, the daylight faded and darkness came as though it had been waiting for his departure. Come daylight he was back again, when he extinguished the tiny flames he had brought to life the day before. At midday, the street corner was occupied by a man with a barrel organ. To a child's mind this was an upright piano with two wheels and a pair of handcart handles. And when the man continuously cranked a handle the air was filled with honky-tonk music. A small tethered monkey held out a collecting tin to passers-by. If any of those men had cast a moment's eye upward to the fifth floor of number 40, then they would have observed an audience of three tiny faces that looked down on them in wonderment.

When Derek Tangye was only two years old, and before his mind was capable of having a potential for memory, his father dutifully volunteered to take up arms in the defence of his country. Colin and Nigel, at the ages of eight and five years, were not able to realise the consequence of their father preparing to do battle in what was to become the first world war – for they only remembered him returning home one day wearing the khaki uniform of an army officer. This was to become a time for change in the family lifestyle; a serving officer, he would not command a salary that was commensurate with that of a City of London barrister.

Sophie and Richard Tangye decided that the household staff would remain, for a while at least. But when the likely moment of adjudication came, it was to be resolved that just the nanny and the chauffeur would stay – and thereafter there would be a monthly revue of expenditure and income. Although it is not reliably known just what his rank or even his regiment were at the beginning of the Great War, Derek Tangye's father was eventually to become Lt Col R.T.G. Tangye serving in the Intelligence Corps. But before that, as a junior serving officer, he offered the War Department the use of one of his two cars; and the Renault Landaulette was accepted for conversion into an ambulance. Together, man and machine, they served among the poppies in the fields of Flanders. Richard was a man of that era in that he had fortitude and he possessed an unselfish sense of obligation to his country and to his king. British and German lives were being sacrificed every day on both sides of the front line. And in those charred fields, where his own life might well have ended in the carnage, he demonstrated the resolve of his forebears in the way they, too, had distinguished the name of Tangye.

4

In the uncertainty and insecurity of a war the scale of which the world had never seen before, Sophie Tangye took her three young sons more often to Glendorgal, the family home of Tangye generations near Newquay. It was on the rugged yet beautiful Cornish coastline where, each new year of his growing life, Derek discovered something further in his ancestral prologue. Such was the impact of Glendorgal on him that gradually he began to think more about its warmth of feeling and idle contentment and less about 40 Bramham Gardens – and although he was born in London it was the rugged Cornish coast that came to influence him the most in his early life. So strong was his bond with Cornwall that, on joining the Duke of Cornwall's Light Infantry at the beginning of World War II, he gave Glendorgal as his birthplace. So it has to be assumed that, at the beginning of a world war, when every able-bodied male was desperately needed in the defence of the nation, if a recruiting officer was told that a birth certificate had been misplaced then word of mouth had to be accepted as a sufficient declaration. Such a deed qualified Derek Tangye to join the ranks of his chosen regiment. If he were to die in the defence of his country then it would be as a Cornishman!

Glendorgal was looked upon as the family seat and it overlooked Porth Beach at St Columb Minor in north Cornwall. An imposing building with many tall chimneys and dormer windows, one of its principal features was a veranda that gave a magnificent view of the small but natural harbour. The house had been purchased by Derek's grandfather, Sir Richard Tangye, in 1882. A proud embodiment of all steadfast Cornish manhood, Sir Richard was one of four brothers who all made the name of Tangye

12

synonymous the world over with hydraulic engineering. Another achievement that was associated with the name of Tangye was that of pioneering a new concept in industrial relations, developed at a time when social unrest fermented on factory floors throughout the land as a result of the oppressive boardroom attitudes of the day.

The engineering works was established in Birmingham, but it was Cornwall where Sir Richard was at home, and he purchased Glendorgal to serve as a kindred sanctuary for himself and for the family who would follow him. It was also within easy reach of his own birthplace at Illogan near Redruth. The property was later to come into the ownership of Derek's uncle Sir Lincoln Tangye, from whom it was purchased by his father, Richard.

The nursery at Glendorgal was less comfortable than its crow's-nest equivalent on the fifth floor of 40 Bramham Gardens in Earls Court. The Cornwall room faced north, which allowed the winter wind to transfer its cold by penetrating the glass of the only window in the room – a window that was four feet from the floor and thus denied any curious child the satisfaction of looking out. The nursery was used, therefore, mainly in the spring and summer – winters were still being spent in London. A solemn-looking oak cupboard, removed from Bramham Gardens, almost concealed one wall of the nursery and on it, in bleak letters, were painted words that the three young brothers were never to forget: *Labour warms, sloth harms.* It was Derek who would find it the most difficult of all to heed such a warning in his early manhood. The cupboard was to leave the family ownership more than 80 years later when, in April 1997, it would be sold in a sale of possessions following Derek Tangye's death in 1996.

As 1914 began to draw to a close, the war intensified and news reached the War Office that a single German U-boat had sunk three British Navy cruisers with the loss of 1500 men. And the battle's tentacles reached out from the watery

13

graveyard of the Atlantic Ocean and the massacres of the poppy fields of France when, for the first time, enemy bombs fell on London. In 1915 the war was costing the nation £1 million a day and Lloyd George imposed a levy on every pocket and wallet by doubling the rate of income tax. The Tangye family finances came under an even greater strain.

With the Renault Landaulette serving the British fighting forces as a converted ambulance in France, the remaining car was used by the chauffeur to drive Sophie Tangye and her three young sons to Glendorgal each festive and holiday season. But with the introduction of petrol rationing, once in Cornwall, the car was used just occasionally; picnic places, on warm summer days, were reached by the use of a jingle (a Cornish pony and trap). This was hired in the same way as a taxi is today and country places like St Mawgan were visited, with a picnic basket crammed with enough food for a hungry family of three growing and energetic boys. Memories of Perranporth were filled with the taste of delicately sliced cucumber sandwiches that crunched as the teeth bit into the tiny grains of sand that had somehow found their way between the slices of bread. Generous Cornish cream teas were addictive when eaten at a rustic table on the lawn of an old stone cottage.

Sophie Tangye was careful never to show to her young family her concern for the safety of her husband as she continuously looked for news of him from the battlefields of France. As the war progressed, with the activity of the German U-boats in the Atlantic Ocean hunting out allied supply shipping, it crept into Cornish coastal waters where the young Derek and his two brothers witnessed the sinking of a merchant ship. Holed by a single torpedo, it slid vertically and stern first to join the ancient wrecks that already rested peacefully on the seabed. In the first six months of war Great Britain suffered the loss of 104,000 of its prime young manhood: each one a son and brother and many, in addition, a husband and father – by the following November the war casualties numbered 510,000. In December another 25,000 were to die in the battles that raged at Anzac and Suvla. As the news continued to reach the home front it seemed that no soldier, British or German, could survive such a holocaust – and families lived in fear of receiving a telegram from the War Office.

Sophie Tangye now began to prepare herself for what she was convinced was an inevitable outcome. Her sons were too young to understand just what such a war was all about but, nevertheless, Derek sensed in his mother a strength that assured him in his own need to feel secure – a trait he would, one day, instinctively recognise in someone else when maturity would nudge him to select a marital partner.

Cornwall had an influx of walking wounded from the battlefield of Mons, in France, and the more seriously injured and the mentally distressed convalesced there also. It became commonplace to see so many soldiers, some no more than 18 years of age, adjusting to a life ahead with a limb missing. Many were invited to Glendorgal, where they arrived wearing "hospital blues" in a temporary exchange for their khaki uniforms. They sat on the veranda looking out on the peace of the rugged Cornish coastline and enjoyed afternoon tea with the family. And as Sophie Tangye listened to the horrific tales that some had a compulsion to tell, she struggled even more to conceal the deep concern she had for her husband.

God, in a mercy that was difficult to understand in that he should spare the lives of some while others had to perish, brought Richard "Gibby" Tangye home to his wife without any injury whatsoever and, in her eyes, he had been blessed in response to her faith. The year was 1918 and the Great War was soon to end but, for the moment, the war was still in progress and he was given just a paltry four days' leave before returning to his unit. They were four happy days of thanksgiving for the sparing of his life – at a time when more young men had died in fighting a war than at any other time in history. To live through such an experience became a strange kind of cleansing of the mind; and life from then on was interpreted in a sense that was not

15

understood hitherto, so Lt Col R.T.G. Tangye decided not to return to a career in the Law Courts. He continued in the army in the service of the Intelligence Corps, to gather information in foreign territories that now had to be occupied for a while – for a period of mental reconstruction – so that a war on such a scale could *never* happen again!

5

The coming of Armistice Day brought with it an even greater need for allied occupational forces and for the next few years the German city of Cologne became the home of the Tangye family. The house at 40 Bramham Gardens in London was vacated. The domestic employees were regretfully dismissed and many of the household effects were transported to Glendorgal, in Cornwall.

Lt Col R.T.G. Tangye of the Intelligence Corps was appointed as a staff officer and given a comfortable office on the third floor of the military-occupied Excelsior Hotel – a building that had been commandeered as an Occupational GHQ in Cologne. An army staff car and driver were assigned to him for his official duties and for the family use also. It can well be imagined how different the family lifestyle had now become. The War Department term of "billet" carried an inference of meagre and sparsely furnished accommodation that had been conveniently requisitioned in what had now become a British army garrison town. But the Tangye family home was, in fact, part of a luxurious six-storey castellated house that was hedged within its own grounds, on Bayenthal Gurtel and the Ufer – a very select locality in Cologne. It commanded a bustling view of the Rhine with its ceaseless flow of tugs and barges – but it was shared accommodation. The house owner was a very successful local industrialist, Herr Strauss. The requirements of the imposed takeover of part of his home determined that the German owner, his wife, daughter and housekeeper kept the use of part of the first floor and all the second, third and fourth floors. The Tangye family occupied the basement, the ground floor, part of the first floor and all of the fifth and sixth floors for the duration. It

17

was an extremely odd situation. Throughout, the Strauss family remained inconspicuous – with just the occasional evidence of their existence through the transmission of sounds. When a chance meeting happened, only a few words were exchanged in a reserved response on the Germans' part.

The Tangye family kitchen was in the basement and the living room was on the ground floor. To go to bed, they had to climb a sumptuous stairway and walk through the Strauss first floor – this meant entering the owner's reception room to access an anteroom, where they were able to use a lift to get to their bedrooms on the two uppermost floors. Herr Strauss's resentment penetrated every cubic inch of the interior of his lavish home, and it clung like an intrusive musty smell. He, nevertheless, remained extremely dignified – even when his privacy was plundered each evening at bedtime – he solemnly wore his sense of propriety close to his chest like a well deserved medal.

Many of the elegant furnishings and the valuable possessions in Herr Strauss's home were inherited through the generations of his family who had gone before. The building itself was listed as being of architectural distinction. But two decades later, as the possibility of another world war loomed, in an act of absolute desperation in the knowledge that as a Jew he was about to have his house seized by Hitler's Nazi persecutors, Herr Strauss set fire to it, making sure that it and the contents were burned completely. By the time Nazi officers arrived only the scorched walls remained – contrasted by the well tended lawns and ornamental shrubs. The fate of Herr Strauss and his family has to be left to the imagination as, many years later, Derek's brother Nigel visited Cologne and asked questions about them, on a trail that soon petered out.

At seven years of age Derek Tangye continued to live with his parents in that strange situation of occupying part of someone else's proud home. For much of that time Colin and Nigel were boarders at Copthorne Preparatory School in West Sussex. At holiday times, the two older boys

18

travelled together by rail from Copthorne to Dover, where they took the cross-channel ferry to Calais and then on by train to Cologne. The travelling was to give them an opportunity to savour the freedom of such independence, for which their mother had coached them well.

In later years, all three brothers viewed their experiences in the city of Cologne as an adolescent adventure. But given the situation of being part of a foreign army of occupation there, they were affected by their privileged lives; and their attitude towards some of the members of the German community was sometimes a patronising one. They were to confess that the special concessions and the immunity from many restrictions afforded to the families of high-ranking officers of the occupational forces of the Rhine, gave them a feeling of childhood arrogance – this was often apparent in their daily expression.

When the Sussex school reopened its dormitories for the autumn term of 1921, one of its new boarders was nine-year-old Derek Tangye – or D.A.T. Tangye as the records persistently showed – who was away now from the web of his mother's influence for the very first time. Now he too would be using Cologne only as an adventure playground when reunited with his parents in the school holidays. As the first term of the preparatory school had started for Derek, his brother Colin was turned 15 and he had moved on, having served his full time at Copthorne. Nigel, now 12 years old, was achieving well there – both academically and in sport – and within two years he would gain a scholastic place at the Royal Naval College at Dartmouth. A fine scholar and an extrovert, Nigel would eventually pass out as a Naval Officer, with honours, and later he would also gain a commission in the Royal Air Force. He would become one of the nation's top flyers and would train Spitfire pilots in the early part of World War II.

Nigel possessed an irresistible charm to most young women he encountered. He had limitless endurance in his attempts to conquer the summit of any of his lifetime's ambitions. Derek was an introvert, and he constantly felt he was living in his brother's cold shadow. He lacked Nigel's confidence and his feelings for his brother were shrouded in jealousy. This emotion was also to become an indelible stain of the mind throughout his life, towards anyone who achieved success in the writing of anything that was similar in topic to his own work.

When the young Derek Tangye first arrived at Copthorne Preparatory School, he was placed in a class that was made up of six other newcomers: Form V1(B) – there were, in fact, a total of 15 new pupils in that year. They were split into two classes with the letters A and B. Brother Nigel, who was still at the school, had the suffix of Senior placed beside his name; and pupil D.A.T. Tangye was awarded the status of Junior. Form V1(B) received its teaching from a disciplinarian tutor, Mr Murtagh, who was able to build on any grounding the boys had been given by their parents. With a father who always struggled to express himself emotionally and a mother who did not recognise, or acknowledge even, the principle of defeat, the bleak sentiments of a disciplined boarding school did not cause any of the brothers to seek solace in shamming sickness or to defiantly challenge the school's authority in any way. In this they honoured their mother and their father's name.

But once Derek was over the threshold of Copthorne school he felt vulnerable in the absence of his mother. She had inspired him from as far back as his earliest memories in life with her ceaseless flow of mental energy and enthusiasm for all things. Many of the personality traits that his brother Nigel had freeloaded, as well as those he had inherited, were from his mother; but his were brashly extrovert. Nigel thought little about his own image in the eyes of others – Derek, on the other hand, became sensitively aware of his.

The doors of Copthorne Preparatory School were first opened to pupils in 1903 by its owner and headmaster, Mr Rendall. By the time of the arrival of D.A.T. Tangye (Jnr), many of its scholars had already distinguished themselves in careers that had taken them to diverse parts of the British

20

Empire. Old boys who had achieved position and respect as distinguished members of society were always well received on a return visit to Copthorne. They were an inspiration to younger pupils and a gratifying "pat on the back" to the team of form-masters in a job that had been well done. To Mr Rendall, a good and sound education depended on an ability to accept discipline and that, in turn, was built up through a rigorous participation in sport. He was convinced that anyone with a fair sense of play on the sports field would have a potential of becoming an ambassador, anywhere abroad, for Great Britain. He had watched Nigel Tangye's progress in this direction keenly.

Derek Tangye always claimed in later life, when writing the *Minack Chronicles*, that in his young academic life he had attained no examination passes of significance and accomplished nothing in sport – yet the September 1925 issue of the school magazine reveals on its front page that, in the Inter-school Shooting Championship that brought 65 teams together, D.A.T. Tangye (Jnr) won his school cup by scoring the most marks within his own school team: 66 points with an average of 44.5 for 99 targets, giving his school the pride of 17th place (the highest-scoring competitors only achieved four more points each).

Then, in the same year, at the age of 13 it was said of him in a published cricket review that Tangye developed good scoring strokes, after which he scored 63 runs in an inter-school cricket match and was awarded his cap. That was an event he carried through his life as a demonstration of foolishness in maintaining a conceited opinion of one's self. The following is taken from an interview Derek Tangye gave this author for broadcasting, on the morning of 9 May 1992:

My preparatory school was in Copthorne near Crawley in Sussex and a very beautiful school it was. I always remember – I can never forget it – in the summer they always had a fair on the heath in front of the school. All the hurdy-gurdies were a lovely sound on a Saturday

21

evening and somehow, always on a Saturday, we were given honey on bread. I can see it now quite freshly, eating my bread and honey and listening to the hurdy-gurdies on a lovely hot summer's evening. And, there it was, I had a lesson on how to behave. One summer's day I made 63 runs for my cricket team and I was awarded my cap. The opposing side was called The Wick, also in Sussex, and a few weeks later we had to play The Wick on their home ground and I was foolish enough to feel frightfully conceited with my new cap and having made 63 runs. I sauntered out to the cricket pitch and said to myself: 'I'm going to knock these people all over the place' – and I was out first ball – I will always remember that!

At Copthorne School it was the headmaster's wife, Mrs Rendall, who determined the standard healthy diet of boiled vegetables and steamed puddings – a daily intake that was very similar to that which Sophie Tangye had always insisted was healthy and which she demanded from her cook for her family. So it was not food that was going to be Derek Tangye's first experience in basic living; instead it was to be the plain walls of the dormitories, the scrubbed wooden seats of the lavatories, inadequate heating when getting out of bed and preparing for a winter's morning run.

In 1923 Derek was deeply saddened when his paternal grandmother passed peacefully away in Cornwall at the family home of Glendorgal. For the first time in five years the name of Tangye appeared only twice in the listings in the summer sporting review of the *Copthorne School Chronicle* – and coincidentally the school had one of its most disappointing cricket seasons. It was also the year Derek said farewell to his brother Nigel, who had passed an entrance examination for the Royal Naval College at Dartmouth. There was now just one Tangye at Copthorne, which meant Derek "came of age" in that he was no longer referred to as Junior. But in spite of the fact that he and Nigel were now separated by a great distance, Derek still felt overshadowed by his brother. Nigel, in his first term at the Dartmouth college, was quick to win two cups for his achievements in the college first football team.

Derek was on his own for the first time in his life – he was 11 years of age and had no other member of his family to turn to. He became more determined and decided to draw strength from Nigel's example. By 1924 he was a Forward in the Copthorne second-eleven team, making positive contributions in the winning of major matches of that year. It was a good Christmas when he returned to Glendorgal for the festive holiday celebrations – for now, at last, he felt he had acquired something of a parity with his brothers.

Derek's year of crowning glory in the field of sportsman-ship was 1925. He was 13 years old and in his last year at Copthorne Preparatory School. He was still too young to understand that he was an individualist and just what that meant. As such, he would find the going increasingly diffi-cult in a way of life that was predominantly geared to a much closer involvement with others who called for "team thinking". Such would be the way of life on the road ahead for him in becoming an adult. In spite of this, he made a much greater effort to become involved with the special skills of teamwork and, for a while, it worked. But he was constantly aware of a comfort of the mind in taking things at his own pace. He felt he worked much better in the freedom of his own individual choice. In teamwork he was compelled to follow a leader with whom he might not agree in his interpretation, and he would be manacled in a dependency on others. If he was able to make his *own* decisions then he need answer only for his own faults. But, unfortunately, the individualist has a tendency to be less vocal in such a situation – sometimes inclined to go it alone by putting his own ideas into practice – almost in opposition. This is often misinterpreted by others as the contemptuous attitude of a cavalier.

Derek's final year at Copthorne Preparatory School was 1926 and he became one of nine pupils in Form 1 under the guidance of form-master Mr Rendall – who was also the school's headmaster and proprietor. The school had only existed for 23 years yet it had a success rate that was already being admired by other such establishments. What could it do for D.A.T. Tangye? Every successful house of learning must have its failures also, and in this Derek Tangye became a noted pupil. There was no lack of effort on the part of all who shared in the task of teaching him and there could be no accusations of malingering on his part, for he really did try. He was a very intelligent boy, but one who did not reveal any aptitudes whatsoever. However, he had a good ear for music and had he shown any talents with instruments then he would have had the makings of a fine musician. Classical music was the one medium through which he was able to express himself emotionally.

Hindsight can often reveal the flaws in the camouflage of youth and an analysis can discover a wrong path that may have been taken. But with the young Derek Tangye there was nothing that was very obvious. Whereas, at the outset of manhood, the new shoots of society can burn with ambition, he had no such feeling. He knew what was expected of him. He often felt like a pear, out of place on an apple tree. He did not understand his own inner feelings and was, therefore, unable to discuss them with others – that was, until the day that Jeannie came into his life; for she had an instinct, so rare, that she intuitively grasped an understanding of him from the start. He did not have the same ready inclination as she, but he was quite prepared to place himself in her hands as though she possessed buoyancy enough to support the two of them.

In that final year at Copthorne, as he attempted to contemplate his future, he had news that his eldest brother Colin had qualified as a chartered accountant and was already making plans that would take his career further. Nigel was, by now, in the final stage of training as an Officer Cadet at the Royal Naval College at Dartmouth and would soon pass out with honours – whereby he would sail the seven seas and develop an interest in flying that would take

24

him from the Royal Navy into the Royal Air Force. He enrolled in an auxiliary bomber squadron that was based at Hendon aerodrome. Then he became a test pilot and trained Spitfire pilots in World War II. He wrote books on flying and reviewed anything to do with aviation for *The Spectator*. He wrote articles for the *Evening News* and the *Observer* and became a well known broadcaster with the BBC.

Derek had the courage that had long been associated with the Tangye name but it lacked definition, in that he was not always sure of what was firm of purpose and what was naive. He also believed that he had an affiliation with destiny as it travelled ahead of him: like a sapper clearing a path through a minefield. Destiny was in the mind and it was intangible in its perception; but to him it was a guardian angel. His mother had always impressed on him that if he wanted God to respond to his needs then he would have to believe that he truly existed before the terms of faith could be discussed. At that stage of his life, Derek trusted his mother's words; nevertheless he chose to put his faith in destiny – reasoning to himself that destiny might well be the will of God.

6

In an outstanding book, *The Story of Glendorgal* (a chronicle of the Tangye generations in their ancestral home) that was written by Derek's brother Nigel, there is an appendix that gives the family history, starting with evidence of a family tree with wispy ancient roots that date as far back as the year 533. But the first actual record of a Cornish domicile is in Cambourne in 1582.

Glendorgal, which was bought as a family home by Derek's grandfather Sir Richard Tangye in 1882, was eventually inherited by Colin, Nigel and Derek, on the death of their mother in 1954. It had already been changed from a family home to a good class summer season hotel and restaurant by Nigel a few years before she died – to give his mother a private source of income. Now Nigel wanted to continue in the hotel industry and he bought his two brothers out, becoming the sole owner. As a hotel Glendorgal still survives today and offers a good quality of service. It has retained its own space, watching over the waters of Porth Bay with a sense of a spiritual incarnation – and remembering.

At the age of 14 Derek Tangye spent an idyllic summer there. He had finished at his preparatory school, Copthorne in Sussex, and was anticipating becoming a boarder at Harrow at the start of the next term. With both his brothers making their way in the world he now had to create his own interests and long barefoot walks on the warm sands of the bay had equally long moments of ponderous thought. Much was about himself – but not selfishly. As he sat on top of a lofty granite boulder that gave a slightly elevated view as far as the horizon, he wondered what was beyond – not just the continent of Europe, but *really* beyond, in China. He had heard stories of opium wars and Great Britain supplying the drug to incite and gain a territorial advantage. Were these tales that were told by mariners and refuted by many honourable statesmen really true? Had the books on history and geography at school placed into the mind a credible image of what really existed? Books spoke the words of famous military battles and of the generals who were the strategists! What about the places that were so remote even the explorers had missed them?

By 14 years of age Derek Tangye had witnessed class distinction first-hand and was beginning to realise how it created social division. He became aware of the existence of a segmentation in politics, and religion also; and he sometimes struggled to pull the strings together in a mental balance of such knowledge – one day he would set forth his own ideas in a homespun brand of philosophy. As he sat on top of the rock his mind was like a beacon reaching out and sweeping the horizon. Also beyond, there were ordinary people no one had ever heard about. No one had heard of him but that seemed all right for the moment because, at 14, he did not yet know himself.

When he finished with Copthorne School he never paid a return visit; but its memory was to stay fondly with him for the rest of his life. As he left at the end of his final term he made a mental note of its parting image. The grass was neatly cut in a series of wide bands and each led the eye to the shade beneath a line of green trees on the far side of the lawn. The practice nets for cricket still remained in place on the sports field, waiting for the groundsman to store them away until the beginning of the following season.

The school's location was then more rural than it is today. Just a short distance from the busy M23, it still manages to hide within a pocket of nature's protective apron – the noisy traffic unable to penetrate its peaceful repose. Not even the discordant sound of thrusting jet engines, that lift the modern skyliners off the runway at nearby Gatwick International Airport, seems intrusive. Although the building itself has undergone some renovation internally, to step inside is to still be able to savour some of the original atmosphere that has clung fast; and it is not difficult for the mind's eye to recapture the image of D.A.T. Tangye (Jnr) sitting at one of the desks. As a school with a progressive curriculum, Copthorne is now co-educational and the expressive faces of the young pupils in study is a statement the founding owner, Mr Rendall, would be extremely proud of were he still around.

The heath where Derek Tangye once stood eating his bread and honey as a boy, listening to the hurdy-gurdies and watching the spectacle of the travelling funfair, is now quite wooded. But with the coming of today's new generations of pupils, there is now a desire to find an outlet of enjoyment in the field of visual electronics – nevertheless, if the hurdy-gurdies were to pause for a while, just once more at Copthorne, the boarders would still have that same sense of intrigue and fascination that Derek and his classmates once knew.

Researching a book such as this has many pleasures and often there are surprises. When Copthorne Preparatory School was first approached by this author, the principal and staff were not aware of Derek Tangye as a writer and of his worldwide success. They were, indeed, proud to have yet another name of an "old boy" who had achieved fame and they were keen to assist by searching through the school's musty archives. Ancient stone steps were carefully descended to enter a dungeon-like chamber – and in doing so it was requested that feet were stamped loudly to frighten away any trespassing mice. There were slatted wooden shelves, many festooned with abandoned spindly cobwebs that clung to boxes of old papers and documents. After the hunt began, the first name to come to the fore was that of Nigel and, although the two brothers were close in their love for each other, the evidence suggested that he and Derek moved independently within their own age groups. Nigel was immensely popular with the other boys, while Derek chose his friends carefully.

The cool stone and brick chamber had originally been

used to store fruit from the school's own orchard and vegetables from the kitchen garden, but it had become a preserving chamber of a different kind – one that conserved time. It is probably the only part of the school that still looks exactly as the Tangye brothers would have remembered, had either of them returned.

As Derek aged beyond the years of maturity, his values remained strongly traditional. His principles were as clear as crystal; but in his chronicles they sometimes became conveniently fogged if writer's licence was needed. He lived in a changing world and was reluctant to be carried with it in its questionable progression. There were not many people he truly admired and he was intolerant towards those he saw as halfwits. But he applauded the achievers in life – especially if they had to climb out of a pit with slippery sides to do it. It mattered not that they opposed his own particular bias – if they showed strength and courage then he shook their hands.

One of the first people to ever impress him was already being commemorated when he arrived at Copthorne School. A former pupil, Edward Wilson, died with Captain Scott at the South Pole in 1912 (the year Derek was born). And often during the Sunday morning service in the school chapel Derek would ponder the stained-glass memorial window and a picture that carried the adventurer's name that hung on the wall. His heart became lifted, not saddened, because he knew it was the nature of the adventure in this man's death that had immortalised him. Edward Wilson gave inspiration to the young D.A.T. Tangye as he knelt on the hard floor of the chapel. The palms of the youngster's hands were pressed together, one eye half-opened and looking at the window. Derek could not see himself as a pupil who would one day be displayed in the school in a way for all to know of. But as a result of the writing of this book, that is what in fact has now happened.

When Derek left Copthorne Preparatory School at the age of 14 he took the road to Harrow. It was also the year in which Queen Elizabeth II was born, almost as an outsider

29

to the throne, at 17 Bruton Street in London to the Duke and Duchess of York. In literature, A.A. Milne published *Winnie the Pooh*.

The occupation of the Rhine by British forces came to an end and Herr Strauss's house in Cologne was de-requisitioned. Lt Col R.T.G. Tangye returned with his wife to live once again in Britain and they leased a house in London. Glendorgal in Cornwall had been rented out in their absence abroad, having provided a private means to boost an army officer's salary – but now they would need it once again.

In his moments of contemplation, Derek became aware that he was not a competitive type of person. He felt no motivation for gaining supremacy in a direct challenge over another human being. Maybe he was sensitive to defeat – at 14 years of age he could not be sure. He did, however, envy those who were able to strongly contest something they desired. It was his experience at school that those who were highly talented in sport were also somehow blessed with a fine, developed body, good looks and a rugged charm. Or was it that the mind impressed them on others in that way? They also seemed to possess an unshakeable confidence – something Derek lacked in himself. But it was pertinent to him that if he were to keep his faith in destiny, something so intangible could never be questioned; and that would be equal to almost anything that the sportsman could possibly achieve.

Derek Tangye knew that wherever he may travel in the world, as with his two brothers, the long road home would always end at Porth beach where, twice each day, the sand was washed like satin by an incoming tide. The bay harboured memories of past adventures and now, as he was growing up, it became a place of freedom for the mind also. All his life, in the spirit of his childhood recollections, he ran gleefully with Colin and Nigel, along the coastal path to a place known as The Point. There they watched small black coasters labouring, each with a belly full of coal that was destined to fuel the steam winches of the Cornish tin mines. The dumpy vessels navigated the bay to finally beach themselves below the high tide line – and there they waited as their cargoes were transferred to lumbering horse-drawn carts. When discharged, they remained like stranded whales to be refloated on a following high tide.

Cornwall was, indeed, the cradle of his kismet and he enjoyed, immensely, that summer of 1926 at Glendorgal. And as he did, seven-year-old Jean Nicol and her sister Barbara were holidaying beneath that same blue sky, not many miles away, with their parents at Bryher in the Scilly Isles.

7

Each one of the three Tangye brothers possessed a fertile mind and they viewed their father as a wizard of constant intrigue. His indulgence in all that was newly developed, both electrical and mechanical, fascinated them constantly. He built his own crystal wireless set and sat for many hours with a bakelite headset clamped tightly to his ears, while he tickled the "cat's whisker" in contact with a crystal and tried to make sense of a poor radio signal that crackled uncomfortably with atmospherics. As the primitive technology was to improve, a bewildering collection of artefacts became the result of his enthusiasm, and he accumulated many polished brown wooden boxes and cabinets; each contained a circuitry of cumbersome components that were soldered together on insulation boards and attached to a metal chassis. There were sturdy knobs that rotated coarsely calibrated dials, and horned loudspeakers that emulated the hollow sound of an empty biscuit tin. Large thermionic valves had fine wire filaments that were confined within vacuum-filled glass cases and they glowed with enough electrical energy to be too hot to touch. There were large handwound coils on bakelite formers to select and receive alternative broadcasting frequencies. Anyone who did not begin to understand the new world of the wireless set simply allowed its mystique to wash over them – and they enjoyed its magic without question. Concerts were transmitted live from London and were received through the courtesy of a length of aerial cable, many feet long. This was an antenna that was stretched like a high washing line between two upright poles in the garden and was isolated at either end by porcelain insulators.

But for all the fascination he discovered in his father's

ways, it was his mother who continued to inspire Derek the most – for he was not technically minded like his father and brother Nigel and he showed no such aptitude.

As a barrister, Richard "Gibby" Tangye was unable to return to his profession. He no longer possessed a level of competence that was commensurate with the constantly changing requirements of the laws of the land. There had been many amendments and new introductions through parliament which made the task of catching up an extremely difficult one for a man of his age. And although Derek was his only dependent child now, there became a need for a much tighter economy within the family budget. He decided that Glendorgal should be rented out once more. It was a property with character and set in glorious Cornwall – a combination that would appeal to many who lived up country and who were in need of a temporary environmental adjustment. So, for the time being at least, the Cornish family home was to become Cavern Cottage, a modest dwelling that was situated between the bays of Porth and Watergate – for which the rent they paid was but a token of the income that was collected from Glendorgal.

Those were, indeed, very worrying times and it was a vacuous whim of the mind of youth that not one of the three sons felt concerned to witness their father as he sat, at the bureau in his study, with the constant lines of stern regard on his face. It became a year of mixed blessings for, disregarding a need for greater income, Colin was still achieving as an accountant and Nigel was close to gaining a commission in the Royal Navy. Derek's place at Harrow was secure and waiting for him – but at 14 years of age he was still to reveal a talent, an aptitude, or even an inclination that would give an indication of a future that might wait patiently for him somewhere.

The year 1927 saw Derek Tangye settled well into the seat of learning at Harrow and, although willing to try, he still could not discover the seed of any ambition within himself. It is not known exactly how he gained a place at Harrow – the college searched the archives but was unable

33

to discover any document of eligibility. It was likely he sat an entrance examination based on his knowledge of the arts, which was one of the qualifying requirements of the time. In this direction his mother had schooled him well, right from the nursery. The arts embraced one or two fields in which he had shown moments of promise and hope, yet it seems no academic tutor recognised this and led the way for him. His life, in retrospect, shows that his mind did not possess the sharp, calculating sidestepping of a politician or even a car salesman; nor did he have the skilful hands of an engineer or furniture maker. But he *did* have a capacity for abstract thought, for he was later to demonstrate how he could take the prosaic realities of everyday life and reinterpret them in a way that gave life to dead wood – and maybe added a few artificial leaves as decoration at the same time. In the years that lay ahead he was to feel more cosy as a rural Cornishman than as a metropolitan scholar. Mother Cornwall would lovingly open her arms for him at a time when the big city duchess had turned fickle on him. His life at Harrow was even less eventful than at Copthorne – the only nugget of hope for his future being a nurturing of his interest in journalism. He left in 1930 and, once again, he looked anxiously back over a period of non-achieving. There had been no oracle in a cap and gown with any well meaning advice to help him on his way, except one house-master who suggested to him, 'Don't be rude to servants in other people's houses!' Derek misinterpreted the master's statement and dismissed his good intention.

At Harrow Derek Tangye was in the Park House Group, and in the assembled photograph for the year of 1927, seven places to his right is Terence Rattigan, who was to become a celebrated playwright. The photograph for the year 1929 shows some of the members of his group as college cadet officers in army uniform. He stands proudly amongst them. He watched most of his fellow students graduate at Harrow, and witnessed them as they enthusiastically made plans to begin training for a professional career. In his own experience he did, indeed, learn much. But when it came to

34

recalling knowledge, as he sat at an examination desk, he developed a mental block that caused him to flounder for words – which was curious because destiny would lead him to become a prospector who would pan for words, in the running waters of Dorminack, in Cornwall.

As with any generation, there is a need to understand the mode of philosophy of the young men and women of their time and of their writing also – for this will reflect just some of the curiosities of their political and moral interpretation and reveal something of their social thinking. Many of their liberal thoughts were to set standards that still influence the basic attitudes of many men and women today. But Derek suspected these people of being manipulative and he stood well back from them. When he left Harrow he knew it would be expected of him that he would earn his living and have his own accommodation – and that he should walk in his own shoes. Nevertheless, it was comforting for him to know that his mother and father were living in London once again.

He became a lodger at 38 Cranley Gardens, just off the Bromley Road: a little over half a mile from the Royal Albert Hall and the Victoria and Albert Museum. To the west, in close proximity, was 40 Bramham Gardens – his birthplace. He rented his privacy now in an arrangement of two top-floor rooms with a bathroom and a gas-operated geyser that took one shilling in a meter and gave piping hot water at a moment's notice. 1930 was an interesting year to be 18 years of age – especially in London. It was announced on the wireless and in the newspapers that Frank Whittle had invented the jet engine; the nation was proud and Nigel Tangye was quick to realise its full impact on the future of aviation. Amy Johnson took off from Croydon airport on her solo flight to Australia – and the nation was proud once again when she arrived there safely. Noel Coward wrote *Private Lives*, a play that Derek made a very special effort to see – more than once.

It was to be a summer that Derek Tangye treated as an extended school holiday, making no immediate effort to obtain work. He continued to be a cause for concern to his parents as he drifted in his lack of ambition. He was attracted to a life on the socialite scene and, with some effort on his part, he became a "Deb's delight" and attended the debutantes' coming-out ball of that year. Brother Nigel was already a part of that privileged calendar – but had become bored with the constant smile of decorum and the feigned sweet manner of many chaperoned partners he had tried to woo. After leaving a Mayfair party, Derek would stroll in the small hours among the lamplighters, the milk-men, and the street-cleaners, back to his lodgings in South Kensington to sleep off the effects of too many glasses of champagne – often until gone midday.

That summer was an idle one for him and he became a lover in its caress. Each day was without responsibility. He was free of the shackles of convention. During the day much of his time was spent on his own – and that was of his own choosing. It gave him the time that he needed and, as the *Minack Chronicles* would one day reveal, it also gave him the space in which to contemplate his anticipation of the years ahead. Although his father was supporting him financially during his unemployment, Derek realised he needed to keep a disciplined eye on his spending. He quickly discovered that the more West End social engage-ments he had on his calendar, the less it cost him to eat elsewhere. His accommodation was well placed, which meant he could save the cost of public transport when, on a warm summer's day, he would walk to Kensington Gardens or laze beside the Serpentine in Hyde Park. As a pseudo-socialite he felt privileged. He was aware of a sense of stimulation when in the company of the opposite sex – and he longed for a relationship.

He had grown up in a male-dominated family and he was curious about the mysteries of the female body – he only knew of its contours, for he had never seen a woman naked. His own body was lean with obvious muscle but, although it seemed acceptable to many of the girls who knew him, puberty had left him unsure about the frame that he saw

36

each day in the bathroom mirror. His approach to a girl who attracted him was one of reserve. He would compose many overtures in his mind and when it came to the moment of proposition he would falter for fear that his intention would be misinterpreted.

As a cadet officer at Harrow, Derek had fleetingly considered a career in the army but he had quickly disregarded such a move, because he knew he would be unable to successfully sit an examination to gain a commission. An individualist can feel many frustrations in a modern society. There exists a straightjacket tied around a mind that can become rebellious if it is denied enough freedom in which to express itself. But this has its compensations also, because the persons concerned can enjoy their own company and not feel a desperate need to be part of a social clique. Often seemingly distant from others, Derek could still be a good communicator when there was a need. He interpreted the teamwork syndrome as belonging to the big brother faculty. He saw these people as mentally blocking the actions of their own desires with words that excused their lack of courage to go forward. Leaving behind a discontented life in London would be easy for him, when the time came. In reality, it was the stifling minds he needed to escape from and not so much the city.

When *A Gull on the Roof* was published he unwittingly became a "people's psychologist". He helped his readers to exercise their fantasies mentally and to escape their frustrations for an hour or two each day, as they lingered over a cup of coffee while turning the pages. And from then on, for as long as it took to read one of the *Minack Chronicles*, he showed them how to become an individual in their own right and invited them to live alongside him and Jeannie in those remote Cornish clifftop meadows. That first book opened the mind like a secret door and left it ajar ready for the reader to take yet another look. Utopia is a place of the mind and quite impracticable – Tangye's Minack was real. Utopia contains an ideally perfect social and political reform

– Tangye's Minack was not dependent on such ideals, for there was no overseer.

In 1930, when Derek Tangye was desperately seeking an early understanding of himself, he read Marcel Proust and other philosophers – but always returned to Proust, to whom he found he could relate much better: or possibly Proust had set forth theories that rationalised and justified Tangye's own excuses for himself. At that time, Derek carried with him a constant awareness of class and image. Wisdom, through experience, was still out of reach but he sometimes wondered if he might dare to approach it through writing. He tended to be a serious-minded young man and, at 18 years of age, such a quest for knowledge spoke well of him.

Often, as a deb's delight, he would lie in bed with the curtains pulled to block the midday sun, having woken from a sleep that restored just some of the spirit of the previous late night and, once again, he would contemplate the possibility of a career. But his thoughts were, all too often, inclined to drift into a daydream. His mother had paid for him to study journalism in the form of a correspondence course, and when he was asked by a girl at a party about himself he found it was somewhat impressive to say he was "in journalism".

As a former barrister and a lieutenant colonel in the Intelligence Corps, Derek's father was well connected and was able to place his son in employment, in the junior position of an office boy, with Unilever the manufacturer of soap products. The place of work was Blackfriars House on the Thames Embankment. The wages were meagre but such a company, prominent in its field, gave an excellent opportunity of a career with a dependable future. In cold reality the job gave him the immediate status of a general factotum, making tea and running errands.

Derek now had a future to contemplate that seemed somewhat dismal to him. He tried to convince himself that it was a vital link in his destiny. He was dutifully informed that, after sufficient training and experience, he would have the prospect of being promoted to the position of a regional travelling salesman. This alarmed him because, as such, he saw himself humping a case full of samples on board grubby railway carriages, touring grimy little towns and cities to sell his wares like a hawker. Although, as part of a sales team, he *would* be working as an individual – and that was about the most appealing part of the prospect.

In 1930, to be a representative of such a company did have a certain dignified status in the eyes of many. Some of the "reps" were army officers who had returned to civilian life through early retirement. Many had lost their spark for adventure to social drinking and cordial conversation in the sociable atmosphere of a favourite public house somewhere. Such a prospect hardened Derek's resolve to become a journalist and he penned many unsuccessful articles. Writing for newspapers and magazines was over subscribed and he was ill prepared in that he was not yet sufficiently competitive in his attitude for such a profession.

The following year he was transferred to the accounts office with a ten shillings and sixpence increment in his wages. And it was just prior to this that he had his first thoughts about travelling the world – but this could not happen in his present financial state. In fact, such a dream was most ambitious in 1931 because it was an extravagance afforded, in the main, only by the more wealthy. Package holidays did not exist and the only sure way of seeing foreign parts was to join the armed forces when, in any case, postings were bound to be somewhere within the British Empire.

As an aspiring young writer, in 1931 Derek saw the publishing of Virginia Woolf's *The Waves*. A.J. Cronin wrote *Hatter's Castle* and E.F. Benson finally finished *Mapp and Lucia*. It was also the year Piccadilly became illuminated by electricity for the very first time, and it made a very impressive sight, inspiring the frolics of partying in the West End as it came alive each night in a brilliance of decoration and colour. Derek had no prospect, in the circles that he moved in, of being considered a good catch as either a husband or a son-in-law, and he succeeded in keeping the reality of his working status on a low profile. Nevertheless, his lineage was impressive and his pedigree was noteworthy. Although tinged with jealousy still of his brothers' achievements he felt that to boast of them was to his advantage. Harrow and Copthorne also became background anchors to use in conversation and it did not take him long to realise that, like the social companions he was trying to impress, he too had become a snob. He became noticed, even more, by the doting mothers who pre-empted their daughters in handing him invitations to their lavish parties.

The world of the debutante, he came to the conclusion, was as superficial as it was alluring. And he eventually became of the same opinion as his brother Nigel in that, with a potential as a suitor, he would need the key to a vault that contained a collection of fine arts and the promise of an inheritance of a manor house that nestled somewhere on the South Downs. Parties sparkled with gaiety – and continued until the new day started as a faint blush of light in the eastern sky. In that glimmer of early morning Derek sometimes walked the quiet streets of Mayfair, arm in arm with companions, playing a game of light-hearted banter with the milkman and the postman.

Two hours of sleep at his lodgings and he rose wearily once more and travelled to Blackfriars House, having exchanged his butterfly collar, white bow tie, and tailed black jacket, for his conventional bowler hat and sombre black city suit. Now he was, once again, being seen to be that "something in the city" he claimed to be the night before – and as he appeared at his place of work, as a humble clerk, he prayed that destiny would not let him down.

Came the evening, once more he was elegant in his tails, looking tall, slim and handsome. He danced the charleston, in Mayfair, with a girl wearing a flapper dress – and he gave himself to the enticing music and the bewitching rhythms of Ambrose and his Orchestra – Ambrose who played "the sweetest music this side of heaven". He heard the muted trumpet of Roy Fox who led the band at the Monseigneur; and at Ciro's it became party time to step it out to the euphony of Bert Harris. They were happy times because they were without responsibility – times that were addictive.

For a time Derek attended on an average of two debutantes' dances a week, but these were rather formal. He disliked the idea of having to approach a well disposed and demurely smiling young and superficial Venus, who clutched in her hand a small white programme from which dangled a pencil on a thin silken cord – to be told he would have to book dance number nine, as the others were already reserved. Romantic feelings became strangled by such convention and he began to liken the situation to taxi dancing in sleazy places for "ten cents a dance". Nevertheless, he persisted in the hope that he would one day encounter the girl of his dreams: who constantly taunted him as she played hide and seek with him, somewhere in the back of his mind.

Some of the song writers of the day were Noel Coward, Cole Porter, and Rogers and Hart. Their lyrics were on everyone's lips, young and not so young. Derek was weaned on the arias of the opera houses and classical music, but these he reserved for the more serious moments of his life. To become a debutante was a dream of honour for every young girl of a more privileged social class and such a celebration became a spectacle the nation loved to read about, and also to witness in the newsreels on the cinema screens. *Picture Post* and *Illustrated* covered the events through staff photographers. Each girl was taught how to curtsy, for she was obliged to demonstrate the etiquette of the occasion on being presented at the Palace. The young lady may have worn a trailing chiffon dress that was delicate and somewhat pale in colour, with a soft and dainty headpiece that was worn to the back of the head, from which a short thin veil brushed her shoulders. In her hand she sometimes held a large ostrich feather, which had become a fashionable symbol of the presentation.

In the early 1930s the debutante was presented at court in Buckingham Palace. A line of shining black limousines stretched in a queue the length of the Mall and became the object of scrutiny by the probing eyes of sightseers. Onlookers admired the jewellery, the organdie, the satin and the feather boas within each car that, due to the slow process of presentation, had to crawl at a snail's pace to the palace concourse.

The first celebration of the year was Queen Charlotte's Hospital Ball. From then on the season would continue with charity balls and matinees. Famous hostesses held functions in the grounds of their sumptuous homes and Derek's name was on almost every invitation list. He was honoured. This encouraged him in a feeling that was inwardly bold and audacious, forgetting for the moment his lesson on the cricket pitch at Wick near Copthorne. Not until he entered Blackfriars House the following morning and sat at his place of work with a weary mind, was he more humbled once again – and each time he was urged, more strongly, to better himself. He kept a diary, but not always as a true record of daily events. Much of what he scribed was merely an interpretation of his feelings at that moment, of which he was sometimes to form a different opinion later.

The ceaseless flow of traffic outside his office was noisy and it constantly pumped obnoxious exhaust fumes into the atmosphere as it paused every few hundred yards, seemingly to play games with frustrated pedestrians who tried to cross the road. Lighters pulled barges on the river Thames and each boat barked a warning at the other, like a teasing dog, as it navigated the busy waterway between Westminster and Waterloo bridges. Often, as he sat at his desk, Derek looked through the window to the street outside and he saw the frowns of apparent discontent on many of the faces of the pedestrians. His mind drifted to Cornwall, where there was peace of mind, and clean healthy air came off the Atlantic Ocean.

He was a young man of the 1930s and then, as today, all young men needed a goal to inspire them towards a future that would flourish in middle-age fulfilment. But his lack of commitment made him suspicious of any such ambition, because it sometimes seemed to him that employers fed such enthusiasm with a carrot on the end of a very long stick. He felt that, if his time belonged to him and not to an employer then he could probably achieve things in his own way. And he continued to talk to his diary, hoping it would answer him in the way of his heart.

He remembered once, just before leaving his preparatory school in Copthorne, his form-master, Mr Rendall, told the class a little story about a traveller who entered an ancient walled city to do business there and, when he left, the traveller said to the guard at the gateway, 'What a lovely city – such nice people. I look forward to returning again one day.' And the guard said with a friendly smile, 'Yes, you'll find most people like that wherever you go these days.' Then a few days later another traveller entered the city. But as this man left, he told the guard, 'What a terrible place – with terrible people. I wouldn't want to return here again!' And the guard said to him also, 'Yes, you'll find most people like that these days.'

It was then Derek decided to visit a phrenologist at Ludgate Circus, to have the bumps on his head felt – he thought such a person might be something of a short cut in his destiny. When the oracle warned him, after a lengthy exploration of his head bumps, that he must not barter, Derek remained motionless in the chair. He heard the voice once again over the noise of the passing traffic; but this time it was a little louder. 'You must not *barter*!' And when he was advised that among all other skills it was journalism he would be more suited to, he knew he had heard what he wanted. He gladly paid his consultation fee and left feeling that a guiding voice had spoken to him from the wilderness of his confusion.

He returned to his place of work with Unilever and immediately gave his notice. He left the company on 18 March 1934, just 17 days after his 22nd birthday: an anniversary on which he also quit his lodgings at Cranley Gardens and took on accommodation with less ·room but with a greater degree of independence. His new dwelling place

43

was at a self-contained address not far from Sloane Square. Its name gave him great comfort for it was one that was not unfamiliar in Cornwall: Joubert – Joubert Studios.

It seemed strangely coincidental that his mother and father were also renting a house in Cranley Gardens at that same time. He was now, once again, without an income or any other means of support. His parents instantly gave him an allowance that covered his rent, food and spending money. They claimed to understand his reasoning and they supported him in his resignation from Unilever. It seems apparent that, in both their opinions, he was justified in all that he did.

With such overwhelming support from his mother and father, Derek felt that, at long last, the cavalry had arrived and it had broken the siege of his good fortune. Also, the phrenologist's crusading words still rang in his ears. And the wisdom he had discovered in the writings of Marcel Proust took on a renewed inspiration, with an ensuing clarity in its forward vision. Events were now being pulled tightly together by a single thread – that of destiny.

Many years later, it was suggested to Derek Tangye in the interview he gave the author at Dorminack, in May of 1992, 'You have written frankly about the stress of failure and also the frustrations in market competition in selling your crops [a market on which he and his wife Jeannie's survival at Minack depended]. You have made wrong decisions that have cost you dearly – but always, always it seems, you have been able to come to terms with yourself.'

As the speaker finished what he was saying, Derek Tangye was ready with his reply and soon spoke. 'Well, of course I must take you up on that point – it's just that I was influenced when I was a young man by Marcel Proust, who was a French philosopher. He opened my window about how other people felt and I found he felt the same contradictions as myself. Ever since, I've wanted to read writers who, by the end of their book, I have learned something from their lives – and in the *Minack Chronicles* that's what I've always tried to do – I mean – there is the story but

44

there is also the outlet of my own feelings. I *try* to be an enriching experience for other people.'

At the eligible age of 21, Derek experienced the first fluttering of the heart in a love affair. Pearl Argyle was 20. She was a dancer who had arrived in London from South Africa to dance with the Ballet Rambert. But when he first became aware of her, he was sitting in London's Comedy Theatre, just off the Haymarket. She was dancing on stage there, in a revue called *Ballyhoo* – and from the upper circle he became infatuated with her. The softly shaded stage lights constantly blended in a changing of colour, the music was somehow raw to a young man's basic emotions in its pulsating rhythm and he breathed a longing of desire for her. He saw the show several times a week and would return home, unable to sleep. He contemplated a move in an attempt to get to know her. He did not want to become a "stage door Johnny" so he decided to do the next best thing – and he wrote her a letter that was likened to that of an immature schoolboy in hero worship of a stage idol.

It is hard to believe that she responded. In spite of her good reviews in the London newspapers and her potential for greater success through influential suitors who pursued her, she agreed to meet the inexperienced writer of the letter for a pre-theatre supper date. The fact that they saw each other on a more regular and intimate basis was easier to understand because, in life, Derek possessed more qualities than the nature and skill of his letter could have revealed to her – and he was probably more genuine in his intentions towards her than she would have discovered in her other suitors. While it became a whirlwind romance, by inference in Derek's writing of the occasion, the reader is led to believe he lost his virginity to her – one starlit night after they left the Café Royal at midnight and walked, hand in hand, to her mews flat, just off Bruton Street.

8

Richard Tangye and his wife Sophie were able to move back into Glendorgal in Cornwall in 1934, re-establishing it as a family home once more. Times were much happier now. Together, they had painfully witnessed their youngest son wandering aimlessly in and out of worthless part-time jobs that allowed him time to continue his late nights as a deb's delight. An offer had now been made to Derek by a large and prestigious chemical company who sought the services of an assertive salesman. The idea of being assertive alarmed him and the offer was turned down soon after attending an interview at the company head office. Instead, Derek accepted a junior reporting job in journalism. He had the ability to write – now he wanted to learn the art.

His brother Colin had become an underwriter with Lloyds. Nigel had stepped back onto dry land after resigning his commission in the Royal Navy and continued to forge ahead by becoming an accomplished pilot. He had already written his first book, *The Air is our Concern*. He had pre-empted Derek in launching himself onto Fleet Street by writing regular articles on aviation for *The Times* and he was also an air correspondent for *The Spectator*.

Being a deb's delight was becoming uncomfortable for Derek. He was beginning to feel like a manicured poodle who waited on a lead, to be patted gently on the head by the hand of a chaperoned Lady Lucinda, or a Right Honourable Daphne. Such a world of privileges had lost some of its charm and he came to see it, in a manner of speaking, as more of a challenge in an attempt to mislead and impress others. He was aware that, to many of the mothers of the pretty young things, it was an impassive venture of investment for the future, seeking a partner who would give their daughter the best in return as a husband. But, for Derek, it was no longer effective for him to talk of being educated at Harrow – the tie had ceased to transmit its silent message. He wanted to forget the separation of the social classes – this was somehow becoming distasteful to him now. The influence of his breeding had also become a contradiction that he knew he must overcome if he hoped to find a career in journalism – for then he would have to drink from the same waterhole as those he had previously avoided.

During his patchy period of being in and out of temporary work, the government had set up an Unemployment Assistance Board that was founded with means-tested extended benefits. He was humbled in his own approach and rubbed shoulders with modest people whom he came to admire. And he had compassion for many in their circumstance.

In May of that year, H.G. Wells, whom Derek admired as one of the world's most prolific writers, repeated his earlier prediction that there would be another world war by 1940. Coincidentally, a prototype Spitfire was already on the drawing board and being assembled. And as a man who was seemingly blind to the writing on the wall of Fleet Street, that spoke of the possibilities of that war, Derek once again fleetingly considered his chances of making a world trip.

All life must exercise some cunning at some time, in order to survive, and in this Derek manipulated himself into a position whereby he would receive a patronising agreement from Max Aitken to meet him in his plush office in the *Daily Express* building on the corner of Fleet Street and Shoe Lane – almost touching Ludgate Circus where the phrenologist's dingy little consulting room stood almost as a shrine. As a result of that meeting, a fortnight later, Derek Tangye became ensconced in lodgings in Manchester, at the start of a successful two-week trial period, working as a junior reporter with the *Manchester Daily Express*. And such was to be the threshold of a way of life that was commensurate with that of a politician in that, as a journalist, hypocrisy was also an essential tool for survival.

While journalism is seen as a venerable profession by many outsiders, it has to be said it is a highly competitive business where sales and ratings are the buoyancy lines on a vessel that will fly the skull and crossbones should there be a need. Every notable newspaper constantly struggles to retain its reputation to seek out and destroy – often regardless of the cost in personal suffering. And that is where Derek Tangye was to falter on Fleet Street. Journalism has just one face but many expressions, and it works on the assumption that every boy scout who helps an old lady across the road might just be a potential mugger. But in fairness, it has to be said that it also plays a more respected role in society: one that helps to maintain justice with a people's voice – in the carriage of its own political judgement, of course.

Derek found himself in a way of life that was in utter contrast to his previous existence in London. He now saw backstreets at night that were places of drama and suffering. No longer was there the linking of arms with others in carefree song in the early hours of Mayfair. And for the first time he felt physically at risk by violence. He had not experienced before the rusty cutting edge of hate that dwelled within the minds of men and women who failed to recognise the law of the land as a sentinel of a respectable society. Derek now had to make sense of its drama, and to write about it in a plain language that was spiked with tension. No two days were ever the same and he became sucked up into a vortex that was created by a constant challenge. He also discovered the euphoria of a good-hearted slap on the back by the editor each time he made a scoop by treading on the dignity of a poor soul who had suddenly become newsworthy. The effect on the mind became quite narcotic and, for a while, it overrode most of his principles.

He was the one from the big city who should have been streetwise yet, against the brashness of his co-reporters, he felt like a naive simpleton. It was more natural to him, as a humanitarian, to become aware of the little nuggets of good that were discovered buried in the human mire of degradation. But, in a newsroom that never closed, it was sensation in the cast of outrage and scandal that sold newspapers. He was constantly reminded that the delightful stories were for the pages of women's glossy magazines. As one in the midst of a unique fellowship of hardened reporters, he learned something of the value of dependency in a comradeship that closed ranks on all else. He had read Marcel Proust to gain a better understanding of himself – now he needed to read him once again, this time with a mind that considered others relative to himself.

Eighteen months in Manchester slipped swiftly by and he returned to London with a hardened attitude that was now more suitable for Fleet Street. And in his ears he carried the words of advice of the editor from whom he had departed: 'Go round the world before you are thirty.' He was now 25 years of age.

Television transmissions were started at Alexandra Palace in London, beaming programmes to an estimated 5000 receivers, in some of the wealthier homes that were dotted around the city and its suburbs. Nigel was invited to make an appearance before the camera to talk about his role as an adviser in flying, in film making with Alexander Korda on the set of *Things to Come*, which had been adapted from the H.G. Wells book of the same name.

Derek Tangye was glad to be back in London, for he still loved its sophistication as a metropolitan city and its importance as a prominent world capital. He worked for a while for a small newspaper called the *Sunday Referee*, which operated from an office in Tudor Street, just off Fleet Street. Like a chameleon he had changed his camouflage and, instead of a bowler hat and a dark city suit, he now wore an ordinary everyday suit and an opened trench coat – a brier pipe was constantly in his mouth. He was in the spinning hub of world news gathering and, as a young man, it made him feel alive. But he was soon to discover that if he was to be a successful news reporter on Fleet Street, then he would need a determined jaw, more square than the one he wore in Manchester, and the effrontery of an inquisitor – for most of his waking hours.

As a writer Derek was extremely talented, but he had to struggle against the clock when penning the tight descriptive pieces for the press. He occasionally tried writing fiction but, for some reason, it became sluggish in his imagination. However, destiny had taken him thus far – so he continued in its belief. Once again, it seemed a coincidence that Derek's mother and father should return to live in London and this time they rented a furnished house in Elm Park Gardens, conveniently placed in Chelsea. He lived with them on his return from Manchester and he was quick to pick up some of the threads of his old social calendar. But, as a reporter for a newspaper now, he was not to become reinstated as a deb's delight. For, as such, he would have been privy to many personal and private matters of the socialite way of life.

His parents accepted that his work made regular meal times difficult to keep, and they worked to find ways around such an inconvenience. But they resented his inconsideration when it became his social life that determined the time-table instead. He, in turn, became increasingly petulant through their persistence, and he was inwardly critical of their neatness in the house, for he had not inherited a tidy mind. As a barrister, his father's inclination toward detail and small print seemed, at times, boringly unnecessary. So there evolved a predicament where three people, who lived in the same house, were each aware of the other's discontent, but were reluctant to allow themselves to argue about it.

When Derek was later to write the *Minack Chronicles* he was to claim that the decision to move from his parents' home was his; but his mother had already searched the local adverts and found him a neat little mews cottage just a short distance away. It was, in fact, ideal for him and he was soon to move in to a cul-de-sac where old stables had been converted into a neat terrace of little houses. It was a place that had once been home to many of the lumbering dray horses that trundled the streets of London each day, pulling heavy carts laden with wooden barrels that were filled to capacity with a brand of beer that was produced in a local brewery. But as Derek moved his belongings in, with his mother's help, the horses had already been replaced by well polished limousines. The little houses had, by then, become home to chauffeurs and their families. Each day, jacketless, with rolled up shirtsleeves, these men maintained the vehicles in their charge. Children played with skipping ropes, prancing over the old cobblestones. But, with their popularity and convenience of position, the properties rose in value and the families were soon replaced with middle-class tenants who were prepared to pay higher rents.

9

For Derek Tangye during the following year, 1938, failure became counterbalanced with good fortune. He made a triumphant return to the *Daily Express* offices in Fleet Street as a staff reporter – just a little over three years after he had first been interviewed by Max Aitken in his plush office in the same building. Altogether, since leaving Harrow, it had taken him eight years to get this far.

For those who were prepared to believe H.G. Wells's prediction of another world war by 1940, the threat became more positively placed with each waking day. The rumblings from Hitler's aggressions in Europe were now being debated in both Westminster and Whitehall. Sigmund Freud arrived in London to escape Nazi persecution. The British government proposed spending £11 million to create new airfields for the Royal Air Force and an order was placed for the construction of 1000 Spitfire fighter aircraft. In the joining of hands across the Atlantic Ocean, Britain and the United States of America decided on a programme to build warships. And Prime Minister Neville Chamberlain made repeated attempts to pacify Adolf Hitler. On the home front a national register for war service was opened for volunteers, bracing the nation for any potential conflict. And 200 German Jewish children arrived in Britain as refugees.

As a journalist Derek Tangye was well aware of what the events were spelling out, but he was more apt to note the celebrated events on home territory. The ocean-going liner *Mauritania* (sister ship to the *Aquitania*) was being built at Birkenhead; and at Clydebank the liner *Queen Elizabeth* was nearing completion. He also found it a year of outstanding literary merit, as Daphne du Maurier's *Rebecca* was published, Evelyn Waugh penned *Scoop* and Graham Greene caused a sensation with *Brighton Rock*.

Derek's sense of rivalry with his brother Nigel lost its stature somewhat and he felt more able to stand shoulder to shoulder with him in any event that gave a measure of professional parity. One such moment was when Godfrey Wynn, one of the most legendary names on Fleet Street, resigned from writing his lengthy and highly celebrated column in the *Daily Mirror*. Derek Tangye was a popular choice as his replacement: in a change of policy that Godfrey Wynn should not be demeaned by the newspaper by giving the impression he had been usurped by another eminent name. From that moment, throughout the West End of London and beyond, Derek's face looked down from the hoardings and billboards, claiming him to be the newly discovered voice of prudent perception – an oracle of his time. His paper face was thrust into the lives of all who commuted the streets of the city who cared to look up.

Derek's role was to be one of sympathy and support for readers with problems – people who were not too sensitive to see moments of their personal lives starkly bared in black print on white pages. The design of such a column was to have an effect on readers that was quite subliminal – because it was other people's troubles that sold newspapers. He took the column on with the best will in the world – but only after an initial hesitation that was caused by not knowing just how well he could cope with such a responsibility. He was a journalist with a conscience.

The publicity hype falsely informed everyone of his potential to disclose, denounce and condemn. He felt a bit like Lord Kitchener of the Great War, as he witnessed his own fixed expression on a mass-produced poster, demanding attention. Derek was supportive of those who wrote to him with unhappy experiences. For those with a more tragic story to tell he had the authority to give financial assistance. But he disliked the requirement of his employer to capitalise on circumstances that opened up wounds in personal experience. He deceptively showed himself to be the possessor of sympathy and compassion when, in actual fact, at that stage of his life he lacked patience to support either trait fully. Also, as an introvert, he did not have enough charismatic appeal to carry him through any public appearance and was, therefore, not sufficiently theatrical in the way of his predecessor. Eventually he was summoned "upstairs" and, although his column lacked its former impact, his work was praised and approval was given. This surprised him because, as a man who had now become Fleet Street-wise, his employer's response drew no parallel with his own expectations. And the editor's confidence in him seemed even more glorified when he was informed of an imaginative task that was being set for him: To travel to one European capital each weekend to seek a story that was newsworthy in its contradiction. It was an assignment that was extra to his commitment to produce his weekday column. A garland had been placed around his neck but now he was being told he had to earn it.

It is difficult to believe that his superiors could not see that it was an impossible task. The only interpretation worth considering is that of realising, after they had committed him to publication, that although he was a skilful writer he was too sensitive to the sanctimony and duplicity of tabloid journalism – and that did not make for good copy.

His reply must have astounded his editor when he readily agreed to cover such an additional mission and, on the following Friday, he arrived at his office with a small suitcase ready packed for travelling to Paris. If seats had been booked for him on the pullmanised Golden Arrow, embarking from platform eight on Victoria Station each morning for the continent, then travelling would have left little time for news gathering before his return. The alternative would be to catch the train for Croydon airport (the forerunner of today's Heathrow and Gatwick International airports), having pre-booked a seat on an original Imperial Airways passenger aeroplane. In 1938 such aircraft were slow and lumbering early propeller jobs and, in the history of sky travelling, they are now well placed as the "steam locomotives" of the airways. Flying was at comparatively lower altitudes, which did not demand a need for pressurised interiors. Instead, small windows in the fuselage had a tiny section at the top that could be slid back by hand to allow fresh air to enter the cabin for ventilation. Passengers sat in lightweight wicker seats at wicker tables where a steward, complete with a folded napkin over his arm, would serve refreshments. With such technology, Paris was still a long way away – other European capitals were even further.

Unable to resolve the problem naturally, for Derek's tenacity had been underestimated and he had not resigned, the *Daily Mirror* lowered the flag to half-mast and buried the former Godfrey Wynn column altogether. Now, with Derek Tangye back on the pressman's woodpile, his picture was quick to disappear from view on the hoardings and posterboards, and the public was soon to forget the man they had never really come to know. As the result of a face-saving encounter, the newspaper printed a story – one he had suggested to them – that he had resigned from writing the page to travel and write about the world and people he met.

Although under pressure from his employer to do so, he had not, in fact, resigned. And the newspaper felt an obligation to line their handshake with a concealed cheque – as an unofficial termination of his contract. He was now in a position to consider his world trip with a positive mind.

10

To much of the nation in the 1930s the world was a mysterious place. Images of the mind were created from history and travel books and by reading popular fiction. Far-away lands – like remote jungles and deserts – had to be visited through the lens of the traveller's camera and moving film transported audiences by taking them on a journey through the big silver screens of cinemas everywhere. So many were intrigued to learn that Derek Tangye was so dedicated and committed to his profession that, when his country was almost on the brink of war, he should travel the world alone and at risk.

Derek never had noticed the flag of the skull and crossbones as it fluttered over Fleet Street when he had first climbed aboard. Now he felt the profession had let him down somewhat – but he was sure they would indeed be grateful for the well informed articles from a freelance journalist who would write as a special correspondent abroad – so he thought.

As the world waited almost in silence, wondering what outrage Adolf Hitler would get away with next, most travellers were on the move for reasons of business, while others were intrepid explorers or just simply those, like Derek, who had apparently failed in their anticipation of what might possibly be. In Britain there were already people who started to fill up the coal shed, stuff the larder with emergency rations such as tinned food, and buy tape to stick over the windows.

Derek, in his own lack of perception, took such action that allowed him to be a newshound on his own terms and, with a sense of freedom as a freelance, he would no longer be a part of a stifling team. He interpreted himself as a free spirit who would go just where he wanted and would write words to paint reflective pictures that burnished whatever life he encountered. There would be no set pattern to his own life and he would stay in places for as long as there was a need to write. It would be a very insecure lifestyle but he did not see it that way. His security was in the back-up that his parents were prepared to offer – which included the potential of his father travelling to wherever he was, should he be in trouble. He did not lack confidence in himself either – his mother had long since taught him the value of such an attitude as an individualist. And he did not feel friendless in the times that were without companionship – it was only the heart that possessed the potential to be lonely. It was his hope that such a world trip would change his life and establish him, in some way, with a future. In this he was right but not exactly as he had foreseen because, at the end of the journey, he would write of his experiences – this would bring him true and everlasting love from one direction, but an unrelenting harsh judgement from another.

He sailed on the first leg of his world trip to the United States of America by leaving Southampton water on board the Cunard Liner *Aquitania*. He had hurriedly scooped the whole of his life together and crammed it into a sturdy brown leather suitcase. He shook the hands of those on Fleet Street whom he resented and said a sad "we'll meet again" to others. On Waterloo station an emotional farewell was said to his mother and father, brother Nigel, who had brought with him his wife Ann Todd, the actress and star of many films, brother Colin and his wife, and a posse of close friends.

At such a departing, all those who gather tend to arrive early, and much time was spent making small talk, with quips that drew little bursts of polite laughter. Time dragged slowly, prolonging the agony of the parting and then, sud-denly, the moment of leaving came racing blindly from the concourse in a scenario that was one of abrupt movement. Derek jumped aboard the carriage, noisily slammed the door shut and leaned out of the window. A guardsman's shrill whistle echoed beneath the massive canopy of the railway station, his flag fluttered as he waved it at a driver who watched from the footplate. The powerful steam locomotive hissed and belched as it gently pulled its entourage clear of the terminus building. By now, more heads leaned from the opened windows as an array of arms waved silently to those left on the platform. The train slowly gathered speed and, diminishing, disappeared into the distance where the two rails converged into one. Strangely, it was the farewell party who were left to look lonely – their purpose was complete, and they turned and walked a nearly empty platform to the ticket collector's barrier, where they went through to continue the routine of their own lives.

For Derek, it seemed his fate was pre-ordained, for had he not taken this world trip then he would not have written the book of his experiences: *Time Was Mine* – and, as a result, it is likely that he would not have met Jeannie, as one of her many suitors.

In leaving London Derek shed an old skin – in the new one he sensed a changed image of himself. He willingly left his memories behind and looked confidently towards the experiences of the immediate future. But he left debts behind and he was never able to explain to himself just why he thought they would dissolve away if he ignored them. Possibly, he felt he needed every penny that he possessed to secure a reasonable passage of travel and success.

His brother Colin had agreed to sell his luxury Buick limousine for him, as he had not allowed himself enough time in his hasty decision to travel. It was a car that, he had felt, reflected his image of temporary success while he wrote the former Godfrey Wynn column for the *Daily Mirror*. He had enjoyed being recognised; heads would turn on the busy streets of London's West End – often noticing the car first. That was just one of the memories he was leaving behind.

Now, as he waited in a vast customs shed on Southampton docks for his luggage to be inspected and cleared, he felt good about himself. It seemed to him that he was in the driving seat of his destiny now and he could change gear as and when he felt the need. He had high hopes of America, especially New York. Once there, he had the impression he would be able to write of his experiences on Fleet Street and sell to an American public that had an insatiable curiosity about all things British. In actual fact, when it came to it, the average American citizen, it seemed to him, was more interested in Mickey Mouse and Pluto.

On the Southampton quayside a porter pushed his luggage on a two-wheeled hand trolley and led him on a path between cranes that looked like enormous giraffes. The *Aquitania* was impressive in its size, looming high above the customs sheds with a black hull and four funnels, like that of the *Titanic* that had sailed from the same spot 26 years before. Ropes, thicker than a fireman's hose, were lashed to giant bollards holding the vessel firm and fast. He climbed the sloping gangway to be greeted ceremoniously at the top by two smartly uniformed Cunard officers. A steward took his hand luggage and preceded him down an ornate wooden staircase that resembled the wide double stairway of a luxury hotel, and along a corridor until they arrived at his stateroom. As the vessel put to sea there suddenly arose an atmosphere of celebration, both on board and ashore.

As the *Aquitania* made its way past the Lizard and entered the Atlantic Ocean off Land's End, Derek's tall figure leaned on the ship's starboard side and gazed on the distant land of his beloved Cornwall. The sea was slight and the breeze gentle – so different to some of the wild winds that had historically carried vessels uncontrollably to inshore waters and smashed them against the cruel rocks of the coastline, which he now saw through a warm haze.

As one of the "queens" of the Atlantic Ocean the *Aquitania* would enter New York harbour looking regal and impressive. Derek had ensured that he would be almost equally of interest by sending word of himself ahead that was designed to promote him as being someone of importance on Fleet Street. So he prepared himself for radio and press interviews.

At Cunard house in London he had discovered that the

Aquitania was essentially a tourist class liner. He knew it was the procedure that, as soon as the vessel docked in New York, the gangway would be lowered to the quayside for reporters and interviewers of the press and radio to climb up in a frantic inboard invasion, each eager to be first in grabbing the attention of the hottest names on the passenger list. So, in the manner of a celebrated name, Derek booked one of the few first-class staterooms: an extravagance he looked on as a good investment.

He embarked at Southampton on 23 June 1938 and disembarked in New York on 29 June. He relished six days of good food and indulgent comfort. He took pleasure in a gala dinner, having first been greeted, along with the other first-class passengers, by the ship's captain. Mayfair, it seemed to him, had taken to the high seas. There was the same laughing and the spectacle of a fancy dress ball. Drinks and conversation were enjoyed at the bar. There was beef tea mid-morning and China or Indian tea each afternoon when relaxing in a lounger on the sun deck. A steward always stood silently by awaiting a mere nod for his service. It was a lifestyle Derek enjoyed immensely and he foresaw there would be more in the course of his travels. At night, in the quiet of his stateroom, he anticipated the South Sea Islands, where he would be able to relax within a peace of mind that would surely inspire him as a writer. And perhaps there on a sun-kissed and remote sandy beach he would romantically discover a poetry of life that would uncover just some of the riddles of a true love that somehow seemed to have passed him by.

The black hull of the *Aquitania* with its four red and black funnels glided smoothly into New York harbour by way of the wide mouth of the Hudson River and was berthed at pier 94 on the edge of Manhattan: all but a few blocks from Broadway, Fifth Avenue and Times Square – the focal point of all modern youth who had sung the songs and danced to the melodies that came daily out of Radio City.

Derek had expected a welcome flotilla of sturdy tugs

squirting powerful jets of water into the air like huge fountains, by way of a salute. He had also been in anticipation of the sight of the celebrated Manhattan skyline. But in the event it was like looking at a blank movie screen as an impenetrable mist clung to the river and obscured all life beyond it. As the *Aquitania* blasted her horn, two tugs called back in a higher pitch and secured towing ropes aboard, and as Derek watched from a deck above he felt disappointed and somewhat cheated.

Once secured firmly to pier 94 the welcoming parties of radio and press people scurried on board like ferrets. They brought with them the verve and excitement of their metropolis. Their talk was rapid – their minds ever alert. Some of their questions were searching and had not been anticipated by the interviewee and it sometimes took a sharp mind to match with an instant off-the-cuff reply.

Derek Tangye sat in his cabin patiently awaiting a knock on the door by a steward who had hopefully been summoned to take him to the ship's main lounge to be interviewed for at least one New York radio station and one city newspaper – but the call never came. Numerous important journalists had been made aware of his impending arrival, so he made himself more readily available and moved to the lounge. The press cameras flashed brightly – but not for him. Reporters with notebooks in their hands called out over each other, directing questions – but not at him. It did not happen at his hotel either.

The good British writer's copy that he had been led to believe was sought after by newspaper and magazine publishing houses in New York was of no interest. Americans were only aware of the events that affected their own lifestyle and, of course, the dollar. He could not discover any friendly attitude in the average John Doe on the busy city sidewalks. Yet, in reality, he was the resilient type for whom the New Yorker had great admiration and he never knew it – he was the sort of person who could be knocked down and sat upon, only to get back to his feet to dust himself off and carry on once again. London, too, let him down by not always responding to the articles he wrote, that told of the spectacle of American life.

Derek Tangye had stepped ashore at New York with £100 (in dollars) in his wallet. With an average wage in Britain at that time being about £5 per week, that would probably have a street value in today's spending capacity of something like £6000. He had left three times that much with his father, to be mailed to him in small amounts as and when he required – yet he had left debts behind also. The bulk of the money had been presented to him by the *Daily Mirror* in disposing of his services.

The United States became a disappointment to him. He found the manner on the street to be both brash and insincere. Opinions and attitudes could be very harsh and the average citizen voiced an opinion of the potential war situation between Great Britain and Germany that was, to Derek, unreal and out of touch. He found himself becoming defensive and nationalistic in his response. In the city of New York many public service workers spoke in tongues of smart talk and this masked an attitude that would sometimes surface in the manner of cynical humour. This was often a performance that was amusing to the onlooker but not to its recipient. He searched for benevolence in the hearts of New Yorkers and all he could discover was a thin veneer that covered small cracks of insincerity.

Rates of pay in journalism, in his view, were less than what was average for a commensurate job in London. Crime was almost a consumer industry. The city girls were pretty, but they appeared to be aloof. It was, in fact, a city that strongly reflected something of every cool personality trait imaginable. The Tangye dream of meeting the world had got off to a very phlegmatic start.

In his diary he continued to be more audacious on its pages than when in social conversation or meeting someone for the first time. But when a girl took his fancy he became Americanised in his persistent endeavour to get to know her. He had once innocently stalked a girl in London (a practice that was then an accepted boy-meets-girl procedure

62

but, because of its more serious intent now, it is seen in today's society as being a potentially dangerous experience for a young woman). In one such New York scenario his attention was drawn to a young woman as she exercised her small dog on the sidewalk outside her luxury hotel. His approach was one of suave sophistication in a scene from a Hollywood Humphrey Bogart movie – if, indeed, the record of the event was accurate. He approached her with an offer of a drink at the hotel bar, which she somehow found hard to refuse. As a total stranger, and in a matter of minutes, he won the girl over. She was well off, well connected and well desired by other men who had much to offer her. The two saw plenty of each other from then on – in a romantic sense. This and other episodes more sexually revealing, within his travels, became some of the many small segments within the book that he was to write successfully after his return to Great Britain. And it was to be a book on which people were to judge his character and some were to question his virtue. It provided the reader with words of a portrayal of himself that gave some misleading images – possibly through the privilege of a writer's licence. And some of those questionable experiences became a barrier in his acceptance as a son-in-law by Jean Nicol's mother and father.

Being alone in a city such as New York can sometimes be an isolating experience for a stranger. Some of the streets can appear to be inhabited with many surreal images in a fantasy of human life. This an individualist can usually cope with; unless it comes in the form of rejection through manner or attitude. Derek socialised, often well, but he never felt connected. He did manage to get two articles, of 1000 words each, published there. One was about Barbara Hutton and the other about the Duke of Windsor: each feature earned him the inadequate sum of £5.

The book that was a result of his world travels, called *Time Was Mine*, was published in 1941 and was reproduced in 1994 by Michael Joseph Ltd as the first one of three stories of an omnibus edition, *The Story Of The Minack*

Chronicles. It is recommended reading because it is written well *and* with imagination. The reader will follow on Derek's heels as he explains his encounters and his feelings in unusual and remote places, and even romantic moments, enhanced with the colouring of thoughtful hindsight. On the remote and beautiful South Sea Islands, life today has been changed by the shrinking of the world through satellite communications and the sights and sounds of the 1930s have largely disappeared. But read Derek Tangye's words and they come floating back like a bottle he may have thrown into the sea, encapsulating his time there.

When Derek rode out of New York on board a simple Greyhound bus he left behind some of the enthusiasm he had carried with him when he had disembarked the *Aquitania* at pier 94. The remote islands of the South Seas were still distant in his travels – but, as he travelled across America, the long and tiring journey gave him plenty of time to ponder with a heart that was clamouring to be there already. The discomfort of the Greyhound bus journey, through heat and poor vehicle suspension, made the journey feel like being in a horse-drawn carriage, chased by hostile red Indians. Each and every passenger on board was there with one thing in common – simply because it was the cheapest way to travel across part or all of the United States of America.

Derek had stayed in New York for two months, eventually succumbing to the seduction of the spectacle of its constant and vibrant life under the colourful lights of Times Square and the theatrical grandeur of Fifth Avenue. There was an effective manner of irresponsibility and a carefree attitude that magically appeared after dusk, when the nightclubs sprang to life with bright neon illuminations. Now, all that was fast disappearing in his wake as the bus, with its uncomfortably hard seats, sped on its dusty journey traversing America from the east coast to the west. There were whistle stops at places like Cleveland, Toledo, Chicago,

Cheyenne. Routes were taken by way of the Rocky Mountains and across the continental divide, where the rains drained off the land and into the rivers on the west side before debouching into the Pacific Ocean, and rains on the east side became destined to spill into the Gulf of Mexico and the Atlantic Ocean. He travelled on, ever westward, feeling little or nothing in common with fellow passengers – many who talked in conversation with a bias that reflected an attitude in which, he felt, they were blinkered, and many of whom endeavoured, on occasions, to discreetly suck at the mouth of a whisky bottle to desensitise the mind on its long and boring journey. Those people lacked his interest in the countryside that flashed past the window, for it was only what lay at journey's end that was of interest to them. The crowded bus crossed the Utah desert before calling at Salt Lake City, then on through Reno and Sacramento before arriving at Los Angeles.

Although he was still in the United States Derek considered himself, at that point, to be in phase two of his world trip, and he hoped that San Francisco might be, commercially, more fulfilling! Hollywood was a place where money changed hands as sublimely as in New York – like frames of movie film rapidly passing through a projector gate, but still it avoided Derek and he sold very little of his writing. Pretty girls, with hardly a chance of discovery due to the overpopulation of young movie hopefuls, walked the streets constantly and attended public places, desperate in their desire to be noticed by a worthy film producer of honest intent – they had looks, they had style, they had oomph, but not all had a worthy acting ability.

Derek stayed in Hollywood for a month, having spent the previous four weeks in San Francisco. The stay had its good moments, but largely he was ignored by the very people he had hoped would take notice of him. His English accent had little influence as a business calling card; instead, it attracted a negative attitude – this he found was commonplace across the whole of the United States. There were people who were fearful that Uncle Sam was going to be drawn into a war with Hitler if they stood too close to Great Britain. But Derek did have occasion to meet people who were ready to volunteer as fighter pilots with the Royal Air Force after news had broken that Austria had been annexed by Germany.

Britain rode a little higher, for a while, in the prestigious polls of achievement on the North American continent as the Cunard ocean-going liner *Queen Mary* won the coveted Blue Riband for completing the Atlantic west-to-east crossing in a record 3 days, 20 hours and 42 minutes; and the Cunard Steamship Company also launched the world's largest liner, the *Queen Elizabeth*.

A war was already in progress in China, a place already marked on Derek's itinerary, and he was concerned with the recent news that the Japanese invaders had now occupied China's most southerly city of Canton, not very far from Hong Kong's border with China – which was a demarcation line that separated the New Territories of the British crown colony from mainland China. He considered the possibility of changing his route. Four days later the Japanese took Hankow as well – but Derek decided to leave the progression of his journey in the way he had already planned. If he had reversed the direction of his world trip, New York would have been his concluding stopover and he would then, no doubt, have been received there very differently. The experiences of his travels would have given him some authority with which to write about a world that was caught on a crumbling cliff edge of threatened war. The Yankee news moguls would have wanted to know about an Englishman who was received in Berlin almost on the day before the sun went down. Or how a political adversary from a foreign land was received as he entered the half-closed gates of Moscow. And also just how expatriates from a Western civilisation felt as they continued in their daily lives, living in the Chinese city of Shanghai, encircled by Japanese troops who still allowed them freedom of movement – for the time being.

When Derek Tangye left the United States of America it

was by way of California, where he was able to book a passage on a vessel that skirted the coastline of Mexico, down through the blue Pacific Ocean, to arrive at the canal port of Colon, in Panama. Neither New York nor Hollywood had been quite as he had anticipated. Both the kindness and the consideration he had heard about before leaving London were apparently considered to be human frailties there, and were, therefore, something of a contradiction. He had noticed that local commerce in its advertising for new employees called out, in bold print, for "aggressive" salesmen. No matter what the way of life – it was aggression that won the day in all its forms of competition. It was one of the attitudes of mind he had attempted to escape from in London, and when he had stepped ashore on American soil it was as though he had discovered the very birthplace of such an assertive manner.

11

The port of Colon was airless and humid and by midday the atmosphere was tainted with unfamiliar smells. Law and order seemed to be under a constant threat of breaking down in petty crime – Derek Tangye was thankful the place was but a stepping stone.

The following day he sailed on a south-westerly track to San Cristobal in the Galapagos Islands and from there continued on his journey on another boat that made its way to Papeete in Tahiti. From what his father had told him about his own delightful travels as a young man in the South Seas, Derek had a feeling that he was somehow coming home. And the role the islands had played in his father's life promoted them with a sense of dignity and a feeling of respectability.

The continuing journey was an uncomfortable one. The vessel was a cargo passenger boat and, as such, it had a limited number of cabins available – all of which were already occupied when he climbed aboard. So at the eleventh hour, before putting to sea, he negotiated the indignity of travelling steerage. This in its interpretation meant that he had to sleep on a straw-filled palliasse in a darkened corner of the hold, with the constant throb of the vessel's engines being transmitted through the metal bulkhead. Nights were hot and sleepless and fellow steerage travellers were noisy and inconsiderate. He had spent more money than he had intended in New York and Hollywood and travelling in a pauper class helped to conserve some of the money that remained. He had watched actors like Sidney Greenstreet and Peter Lorre in Hollywood films that were shot on location in places like Colon. And now as he travelled, surviving like the very dregs of society himself, he began to understand, just a little, what it felt like to be a real life subject of such a movie scriptwriter.

On arrival at Papeete in Tahiti, he checked in at a hotel that was rudimentary in both its construction and the services it had to offer. Nearby houses were topped with corrugated metal roofs that deafened the occupants during heavy rainfall. The supporting industries on the islands were vanilla and copra plantations – without these commodities the population would have rapidly decreased in numbers. So local goodwill had survived as a maxim.

At last, here was a place where people were truly friendly – who shared their possessions and their pretty young girls. So it was that Derek claimed to have discovered such a natural resource of the tiny islands – that of free love.

Here were people whose only concern about the outside world was that it should continue to buy the produce of their plantations. They toiled in the burning sun by day and quenched their thirsts in primitive drinking houses by night. Their inclination to ignore the inert drudgery of such a simple but sincere way of life gave them placid expressions and a manner that was as becalmed as stilled water. But, as with water that concealed a heinous creature of the deep, so too they possessed an unpredictability of the mind.

Derek soon learned how to feel something of their contentment. There was no strict regime of society to tell him just what he should or should not do. Little was expected of him. If he chose to make friends and to drink socially with them, they were happy to have him sit with them. But such an association was not accepted in a tourist sense of two drinks, perching on a bar stool and asking questions about their way of life. He was expected to consume alcohol to numb the mind and, although a fine definition of meaning was marred by a language difference, the greater the inebriation the more inane was the response of all concerned – and when two parties of totally differing tongues became drunk, each seemed to possess a strange ability to understand the other through stupefied laughter.

On one such a night, he claimed to have walked back to

his hotel where he went to bed and instantly fell into a deep sleep. On waking the following morning he discovered 16-year-old Rai lying naked beside him – it seemed she may have been younger, he could not be sure. He immediately went downstairs to the reception desk to disclose that he had a young girl in his room, and offered to pay for her night's keep. The clerk was uninterested and merely shrugged off his display of such honesty. He returned to the room and claimed that as she lay beside him, because she was so young and naive, she was unaware of the provocation he felt by the sight of her bare and youthful breasts – and once again the experience is recounted through the ambiguity of an opened window in its authenticity; and the reader is left to conclude just what did or did not take place between them.

He later wrote of Rai enjoying breakfast with him in his room and when she departed he watched her young body, from the balcony of his room, as she walked towards the market place to meet her friends and to relate her experience of him to them. In 1941 when the book of his world trip was published, to write of such an experience was a rare and provoking thing to do; and without doubt it helped in the popular sale of the book. But it also became one of the events on which he became judged – for revealing a part of his personality that was interpreted as being in a state of moral decline.

Even in Tahiti, there was no immunity from the satanic curses of life. For the painter Gauguin, such a retreat was an absolute manifestation of all things that had been an inspiration to him in his life, and he settled there. But he fell foul of a local official who, some claimed, murdered him. This was unproven and it left a big question mark hanging over the cause of his death. His widow, nevertheless, continued to live there undaunted by the experience, and found her solace in the breeding of pigs.

Derek Tangye fell in love, bewitched by a tropical spell that took possession of his mind and made him a willing prisoner on the tiny island of Toopua which, together with the island of Bora Bora, formed just a small part of the Society Islands: just south of the equator. This became a heaven on earth that Derek later regarded as the spiritual beginning in his quest to discover his own Utopia.

Maeva was a young and attractive girl with fine features and a copper-coloured skin that heightened her beauty. She was an innocent with an unsophisticated lifestyle. Her spirit was as free as the colourful birds that sang on high in the trees that thankfully shaded part of the foreshore. Derek lived quite primitively in a wooden structure on the shore of the island – barefoot and with just a *pareu* wrapped around his middle, the nights felt as warm as the day and he often slept on the soft dry sand above the water line. And it was there that Maeva mysteriously came to him one day – paddling her canoe across the water from an even smaller island. He knew nothing about her, nor she of him, but this was not important, as love is the fruit borne of a tree regardless of its species – in the roots of Derek's civilisation in the 1930s, such knowledge may only have caused discrimination.

They swam naked beneath the clear blue water, among the brightly coloured fish, just off the coral reef. And at night they kissed and slept together beneath a veil of bright stars. In the light of dawn Maeva speared fish which she cooked for breakfast on an open fire that Derek lit in a small hollow in the sand. Such a scenario was almost like that of a Hollywood movie of that period and had probably been an influence in Derek's writing of the event. Nevertheless, it was that tiny island of Toopua that he was never to forget because, it was quite apparent, it was a place that God had conveniently tucked away to keep for himself.

He shed yet another skin on Toopua and it was harder to say goodbye to those he left behind than it was when he said farewell to his family on Waterloo Station – his family he knew he would see again. Derek stood like an apparition of Man Friday on the deck of the good ship *Stella Polaris* as it navigated the island groups. It was late February of 1939 and he was viewed as a spectacle, like an indigenous

71

islander, bare-chested and with his *pareu* tucked tightly about his waistline – and he was still barefoot. He strolled the main deck among the jewels and gold trimmings of the wealthy American passengers. He was silent and his mind distant when the sun dipped beneath the horizon; for Toopua was far away in the vessel's wake – and he remembered how Maeva had kissed him a tearful and final goodbye. The memory of his time there would always seem unreal in its purity – and to almost become a figment of his imagination. But now he had been given a vision of just how he would like his life to take shape. A romantic moon hung over Toopua and one day it would rise for him in the eastern sky of south-west Cornwall.

He crossed the international dateline and, in theory, lost a day of his life as the *Stella Polaris* made for Suva in Fiji, where he disembarked. Money his father had sent him was collected from the shipping office and he booked himself into a cheap hotel, had a bath, and went shopping. He fitted himself out with a new suit, shirts, a tie, underwear (he had worn nothing beneath his *pareu*), socks and shoes. Civilisation had compromised him once again and his travels would now take him to some of the more urbanised parts of the world. When he returned to the hotel and put the suit on he felt as though he had donned the uniform of a frustrated and demanding society.

He was soon to board yet another boat. One that would take him to New Zealand where two days' sailing time to the north-west, the Japanese army had already occupied the Caroline Islands. From there they planned to launch an attack on the other groups of the principal Pacific Islands. Strategically they had the Philippine Islands covered to the west, New Guinea to the south and, even more ambitious, the most northerly tip of Queensland in Australia also. Very soon war would encompass the whole of the globe but, before it did, Derek would be visiting parts of the world where, in a matter of months, battles would be fought and there would be no more freedom of movement, except for the fighting forces of the principal nations involved.

12

Derek Tangye was a conversationalist who could draw on an informed opinion of many subjects. In writing, his words were keenly chosen but they lacked an edge of wit. He also had a discourse that was sometimes blunt – often reflecting his mood at the particular time. While scudding the streets of London as a newshound he had become skilled in the art of interviewing people for possible stories and he knew how to draw them in their opinions. In his travels he became fortunately placed to write, as a freelance, on what the people of the world were saying and, equally of importance, just how they were saying it.

He had planned an itinerary that would take him from New Zealand to Australia. From there he would visit Manila, Hong Kong, Shanghai, Tokyo, Korea (not yet divided politically between north and south), Manchuria, Moscow, Warsaw, Berlin, Cologne (where he lived with his family as a child), Paris and then home to London, and finally to Cornwall where he would start to write his book *Time Was Mine* – a book that, when published, would lead him to one of the most extraordinary young women of her time. They would marry against the wishes of her parents – who, by then, would be distressingly aware of the lack of direction in his life and, what is more, they would read of his publicly declared sexual experiences in the South Sea Islands.

The author of this book has the benefit of hindsight in the events that took place in World War II and it is interesting to note those events and their outcome, as compared with the fears and anticipations of people who were innocently involved and who expressed opinions to

73

freelance writers and world travellers such as Derek Tangye.

More than half a century has crept quietly by now, leaving behind a trail of events of high impact in devastation and of sad and bitter experience of war. There *were* good times as well. But, as an older generation fades away so it is left to the writers to seal those memories in the vaults of time. It was Derek's experience in Australia, in 1939, that there existed a much closer affinity and a stronger bond between its citizens and the people of the "old country". They were prepared to, and did, take up arms and, if necessary, die in Britain's defence. They were proud to be subjects of the crown and, as such, members of the British Empire also. But many in today's Australia feel fiercely detached from its former self and it was always inevitable that, as a proud and independent nation, Australia, would one day want to constitutionally "leave home". Derek always knew that cousins could possess diverse attitudes and opinions without losing sight or love for one and the other – and he felt that, like him, they would always be entitled to go their own way.

In Hong Kong, Derek was reminded of Noel Coward in song, as the noonday gun was fired in the compound of Jardine Matheson and Company. And as the sound of the blank shot travelled across the water of the harbour to Kowloon it reminded British expatriates everywhere that it was tiffin time, and they rang for the houseboy. The streets of Hong Kong were a continuous movement of vehicles that skilfully avoided rickshaws pulled by men with sinewed legs and arms, who were clad in sunbleached singlets and shorts, as they took bloated Chinese businessmen or amahs on errands. In Victoria, Derek was quick to take notice of the cricket ground, green and spacious, overlooked by a glorious white pavilion. A match was in progress, and the participants were seemingly unaware of the harsh discordant sounds of traffic that moved ceaselessly around them. They played on with a true colonial grit. To the east of the ground was the naval shore establishment of HMS *Tamar* and its neighbouring dockyard. To the south, Garden Road branched off the tramlined Des Voeux Road and climbed its way to the cool air of the Peak, where the wealthy had been quick to build sumptuous houses. At night those same residents looked down on a million lights that glowed from Aberdeen in the west to Causeway Bay in the east.

In daylight, Derek rode the funicular Peak Tramway and from a lofty viewpoint could see distant patches of a way of life that contrasted with many of the images that he had already taken notice of as a traveller. A smoke haze rose from charcoal fires in vast squatter camps that were perched on hillsides, where underprivileged people lived like ants in flimsy shacks. From such a distance, such homes looked like hutches – and in reality were constructed of discarded boxwood and weatherproofed with a cover of worn linoleum that came from the city dump. Occasionally these camps caught fire and people became homeless. From that same viewpoint he looked northward, across the busy waterway of the harbour, to the New Territories, on the far side of Kowloon – but high hills hid the view of the small villages that were surrounded by paddy-fields. Beyond that was the border with China, where the nationalist army of Generalissimo Chiang Kai-shek struggled to purge the land of occupying enemy troops in a Sino-Japanese war.

When Derek Tangye spoke to journalists on the local English language newspapers, the *Hong Kong Journal* and the *South China Post*, he asked them how the colony saw its fate should a war break out between Great Britain and Germany – and even Japan. He discovered a complacency, as the Chinese population were imbued with a feeling of immortality through the protection of the British government in Westminster.

Daily, thousands of refugees from China scrambled over the border into Hong Kong to escape an advancing Japanese army – an army, they had been told, that would rape the women and torture the men. The irony was to be that, on Christmas Day in 1941, the British security forces in Hong Kong were to be overwhelmed and surrender to the Imperial Japanese army. Singapore fell also and, through its humiliation, Britain was seen to have lost face by those very same Chinese to whom Derek had spoken.

As the leader of the nationalist army, Generalissimo Chiang Kai-shek had tried in vain to contain the advance of the Japanese army in China. He was aware of another adversary, also, whom he had branded as a bandit. Mao Tse-tung hid in the remote northerly mountains with an ever growing band of communist guerrillas. The rebel leader was to grow gradually in strength and the outcome of a world war would, in the years that followed, provide him with an overwhelming peasant following that became big and powerful enough to unite his country as one of the largest nations on earth.

In 1939, before the the world war, Derek sat in the lounge of the Peninsular Hotel in Kowloon, enjoying a drink while in conversation with a Reuters correspondent who was based in Hong Kong. He asked him if China was going to be able to rid itself of the Japanese occupation. The fact was that, as they spoke, the Japanese army was getting stronger by the day and no one was able to predict an outcome – so the reply was ambiguous.

Tangye's China was soon to change, helped on by world events. But, before then, Chiang Kai-shek's nationalist army was unwilling to become bedfellows with Mao Tse-tung's communist guerrilla army in the mountains as a joint effort to rid China of an occupying Japanese army. In fact Chiang had failed to interpret the needs and desires of the peasant masses throughout the whole of China, and in the late 1940s he was to see many of his own followers jump the rapid waters of that human river and take up arms within a growing people's army – an army led by the little man Mao, who fought in the shadow of the principles of Karl Marx.

The Japanese occupational forces, through lack of know-how in modern intelligence techniques, viewed Mao as an insignificant creature with a headless body. No one, at that time, would have possessed the foresight to predict that Mao Tse-tung would one day father a modern China.

The Chinese mind has always seemed a mystery in any

foreigner's attempt to decipher it – but then the Chinese too have similar problems with alien thought patterns. A good example of this was when Derek arrived in Shanghai. An American merchant reflected the opinion of the general Chinese population of that city. His theory was that if Chiang Kai-shek were to return and rule China then he would banish all foreigners from its shores – in reality the opposite would have been true. On 6 January 1950, when the British government officially recognised Mao Tse-tung and the communist regime of China, the few foreigners who were allowed to stay in China were mostly Russians – they were technical advisers and there by invitation. Chiang Kai-shek, on the other hand, would have welcomed the anomalies of free trade through private enterprise had *he* ruled China in 1950.

Derek saw the evidence of atrocities that seemed commonplace, committed against the Chinese by the Japanese forces, and he spoke to people who had similar stories to tell. He considered scratching Japan off his itinerary, fearing that his reception there might be an inhospitable one. But when he arrived on Japanese soil the smiles of greeting were as broad as the rising sun that welcomed each new day. They were polite and courteous people – humble in their acknowledgement of him. In busy Tokyo they were enthusiastic, proud to show him their city. And always they smiled and bowed to him gently. It became quite apparent to him that no one was aware of their sons and brothers behaving so atrociously towards the Chinese. So often in history, a nation has been recognised only by an image set by the conduct of its fighting forces, and such was the face of Japan abroad. And for many years after World War II countless Chinese people continued to express their fear, in mistrust of their former adversary.

Stopping off in Korea, Derek's impression was of a peaceful country. It seemed to him to possess a culture that was similar to that of China. It was a nation not yet severed geographically by an imaginary line that stretched from coast to coast in a division of political ideals.

There was a ten-day trans-Russia journey that started in Manchuria. And this was a bleak prospect with an even more uncomfortable ride, by train, than that of the Greyhound bus that took him across America. But now, in Russia, it was not just an attitude problem that Derek had to deal with – there was one of language also. In Moscow there was an overnight stay at the Metropole Hotel, which gave him a little time to snatch a look at the city and to form some kind of an impression of its citizens. His assessment was that an average inhabitant carried a devalued sense of human privilege on a weary back with rounded shoulders. Not once did he witness a face that was warmed with a natural smile. He tried to engage people in conversation by using sign language and each answer had in common its reluctance.

In the turn of events of the years to come, Derek Tangye, himself a one-time member of MI5, was at a complete loss to understand just how British secret service agents such as Guy Burgess, Donald Maclean and Kim Philby could become traitors to their own country and be in sympathy with such a downtrodden and repressed nation as the Russia that he had once witnessed. He saw them as the misguided products of such political theorists who taught in the British universities of the 1920s and 1930s, whose own unsettled minds had been implanted with the seeds of discontent and revolution at puberty. Derek was glad there had been no such influence at Harrow in the days when he was groping in his own wilderness.

Derek Tangye carried with him a preconceived impression of Warsaw in Poland as being a dull and grey city. Like Moscow he expected there to be evidence of harsh constraints and political repression. Today it is an attractive city, having reinterpreted itself from the animated and colourful painting that he stepped into when he alighted from the train. People smiled at him in their welcome and shook his hand warmly. Music filled the air as kith and kin danced in national costume in the streets. There was no lone face, obscured behind an opened newspaper, to observe his political correctness – as he had noticed in Moscow.

In an attempt to indulge in conversation that would reflect the thoughts of the citizens of Warsaw, he met Alex Small, a correspondent with the *Chicago Tribune* who was staying in the same hotel. But surprisingly the American had a poor concept of Polish minds. As the two men sat on high stools in the bar sipping vodka, Derek was informed that when Germany attacked Poland – and it *would* – it would take no more than five days for Warsaw to fall. Alex Small claimed, further, that Britain and France would turn the war into a long and extended battle and that Germany would eventually exhaust itself. But there was a warning also – Britain *would* be double-crossed by Russia!

History now shows that Hitler discovered Great Britain to be the formidable and determined enemy that he sometimes secretly feared. It also shows that he underestimated the resolve of Russia. France collapsed early on in the war and that was an event that Alex Small had not foreseen. Also, the Chicago journalist had not anticipated that his own country, the United States of America, would enter the war. He would, of course, have needed a crystal ball to have foreseen the Japanese attack on the American fleet as it lay peacefully in Pearl Harbor.

Close to the end of his world trip, Derek Tangye, as a Britisher, took a risk and braved any inhospitable feelings that might have existed in Berlin. Surprisingly he was told by many residents of the capital city that they did not want to go to war with Britain and, as a disclaimer, they made excuses for the actions of their leader, Adolf Hitler. It was Derek Tangye's visit to Berlin that made him finally understand that war really *was* going to happen and his mind became numbed, unable to consider its outcome. He witnessed some of the evidence of the might of the German war machine, and, while in Berlin, he felt very British and very patriotic with an urge to return home nudging him constantly.

But he was unable to leave Germany without first making

a fleeting visit to Cologne, where he had spent much of his spirited childhood – especially during his end of term school holidays from Copthorne. There, the attitude mirrored that of the Berliners. He was alarmed to see how German Jews were being isolated and rejected by friends they had grown up with – and in the very city of their birth. High fashion on the streets of Berlin was smart but sombre in its darker colouring and it reflected the murky shades of war that veiled the mood of conversation in the eating houses.

When Derek arrived in Paris it was in early June 1939, and the mode of light summer dress was in colours that encapsulated both spring and autumn. The ambience contrasted light-heartedly with that of Berlin. As he travelled in a taxi to his hotel, he looked out onto the boulevards and admired the girls' pencil-slim figures beneath their dresses, comparing them with those more substantial on the Moscow streets. Innocent, seductive Maeva, who needed not to cover her beautiful naked body, flashed through his mind – and he thought of his island of Toopua. He yearned to be there once again – but that was in another life, one he had escaped to, and now would remain but a mirror in his mind.

He had just one more stop to make after Paris, before concluding his world trip on the steps of Glendorgal, and that was London. Already he was thinking of the first chapter in his proposed book, *Time Was Mine*. The Paris taxi pulled up before a hotel with a wide canopy that stretched out over the pavement on the Rue du Colisée. A commissionaire tipped his hat and a hall porter took Derek's luggage and led him through the swing doors. When he entered the hotel foyer he saw his mother sitting comfortably in a deep leather-bound armchair. He hesitated for a moment lest his eyes had deceived him. She rose to her feet, kissed him, and hugged him lovingly. There were so many questions his mother had to ask of him. And there were so many stories he wanted to tell her – but some were too personal to pass between mother and son. She, like others, would have to discover them when the book was published.

His world trip had taken 12 months to complete. His travelling expenses had been £502, supplemented by £59 from earnings for writing articles, and gifts received: a sum that would have represented two years wages for an unskilled worker of that time.

13

On 3 September 1939, at eleven o'clock in the morning, Prime Minister Neville Chamberlain announced to the entire population of the British Isles that, as from five o'clock that afternoon, Great Britain would be at war with Germany. It was just three days after Hitler had invaded Poland.

For two months prior to that declaration Derek Tangye was ensconced in Rose Cottage in a tiny Cornish village called Coombe, not too far from Truro. He had the family dog with him for company and together they went for long walks – this exercise helped him to ponder his thoughts as he shut himself away each day to write his book. After two months he had only written two chapters – and these were most unsatisfactory. None of the articles he had produced on his world trip and sent to London had been published either.

He scanned the pages of his diary and leaned back in his chair with his eyes closed in meditation. He tried desperately to relive his experiences in the South Sea Islands and to recall Maeva's sweet innocent face once more – for she had shown him a true companionship in the sharing of their love. He knew that, as a writer, it was not just his words and the way he would put them together that was so important – he had to feel their meaning also, so they could arouse and stimulate the minds of others who read them. He wanted to shock his readers, to provoke a response from them in some of the things he had to say – as a journalist he knew the value of such publicity. He knew also that he had been too honest about what he had reported on Fleet Street and a lot of his embellishments had been culled by his conscience. Now, in writing this book, he felt he needed to pep himself up a bit!

Brother Nigel was now in the RAF and training fighter pilots for combat flying. Derek felt totally unqualified for *any* department of the British organisation for war but, on 31 August 1939, he presented himself at the army recruitment office in Truro and, by falsely giving his place of birth as St Columb Minor, Newquay, Cornwall, he ensured himself a place, as a private soldier, in the Duke of Cornwall's Light Infantry and he was posted to the 4th Battalion. He gave his profession as a journalist. At the age of 27 years and 6 months, he was 6 feet in height, weighed a little over 11 stone, had a fair complexion, and fair thinning hair. He was Embodied on 2 September, which meant he joined his unit from civilian life the day before war was declared.

He had every intention of completing the writing of the book about his world travels. But now, as he blancoed his army webbing and polished his brass buckles and his boots, the future was more unsure for him than at any other time in his life – and he had no way of knowing if his country would survive another major war. As a theorist he became a little confused when he tried to equate the aggressive acts of war with the ultimate survival of all humanity and, just for a while, the very philosophy that had rationalised so much of his thinking for him, flew out of the very window that Marcel Proust had opened in his mind.

He was assigned, as a private soldier, to patrol a part of Falmouth docks where ship repairs continued on the same peaceful projects that he had always known there. Very little was happening on the home front and at that very early stage, the conflict was dubbed the "phoney war". In Cornwall there existed a silent patriotic resolve although the presence of war seemed not to exist – it was as fictitious as the comic opera *The Pirates Of Penzance*. And as the sun continued to shine in a blue sky it was hard to believe that one nation was about to savage another.

In that dormant state, when Derek was "stood down" from sentry-go, he used his official rest periods to sit quietly in his car with his typewriter balanced on his knees. He tapped his fingertips on the keypads with a sound like machine-gun fire and, at long last, the book he was writing about his world trip was taking shape.

In the army he had more going for him than he had previously considered. First there was his training as an officer in the Harrow cadet unit of his school year, in which he had shown an ability to have responsibility – but without authority (a trait that was to harden much later, but only through arrogance, for he was not authoritarian by nature). He had to his credit the observations and conversations in those places in the world that had now become vital territory in the strategy of an ongoing war – and of course it has to be considered that his father, Lt Col R.T.G. Tangye (now retired), himself a former serving officer of the Intelligence Corps, presented his youngest son's case for a commission through channels that led him to the War Office.

On 21 October 1939, Derek Tangye was appointed to an Emergency in the General List as a 2nd Lieutenant. Within four days, on 25 October, he was promoted to a General Staff Officer III as an Acting Captain. On 13 July 1940, he became a Temporary Captain and was posted to the London District Reception Depot, and on 19 August was attached to MI5 at the War Office in Whitehall for duties as a Regional Liaison Officer. He remained at the War Office, having being transferred to the Intelligence Corps on 23 April 1941.

In the summer of 1940, Captain Derek Tangye, as a Regional Liaison Officer, was unsure of the significance of his duties in the War Office. He was unhurried by his superiors whose own responsibilities were sometimes unclear to him also. It seemed that doors kept opening and shutting with muffled voices behind and only occasionally was his opinion sought – to be almost immediately discounted. It was an establishment in which it was difficult for him to discover any friendships of meaning. His brother Colin spoke fluent German and he worked in the War Office also, occupying a room down the corridor and just a

Jean Nicol Tangye's sister, Barbara, visits Dorminack

A previous visit - as younger women

Jeannie in the garden at St. Albans aged 16 years

A photograph of Jeannie taken in hospital shortly before she passed away. This picture was loaned for publication by Nursing Sister Margaret Davies, who appears with her, and with the blessing of Jeannie's sister, Barbara.

Derek Tangye poses with the writer, David Power.

Minack after Derek's passing - overgrown

Copthorne Preparatory School where the young Derek Tangye was once a boarder

The 1927 year group at Harrow. Derek Tangye is in the back row second from the right - Terence Rattigan (playwright) is in the back row seventh from the right. (By kind permission of the Keepers and Governors of Harrow School)

The 1929 Officer cadet group at Harrow. Derek Tangye is second row from the back, and fourth from the right. (By kind permission of the Keepers and Governors of Harrow School)

The conservatory where Derek once sat and talked to visitors

Jane Bird and her partner Peter Clough, who now live in the old cottage at Minack (Dorminack)

The Savoy Standard

IT'S HARD TO MAINTAIN, BUT WE DO IT!

No. 1   LONDON, THURSDAY, NOVEMBER 27, 1941   PRICELESS

THANKS GIVEN FOR LAUGHTER

Mr. DEEDS FINDS WAR HUGE FAKE

Knocked out in Blackout
Fingers Way Through Dark

by Robert Riskin.

Dear Ma:

The whole thing's a fake, Ma. The most colossal, stupendous, Barnum and Bailey fake that was ever pulled off on an unsuspecting guy.

Six thousand miles I travelled to see it, feel it, be part of it. I got myself a tin hat and a gasmask. I was ready. Ready for the works! Bring on your blitz, I said, bring on your bombs! Guess I shoulda listened to you, Ma. You were right. The whole thing's a newspaper stunt.

I haven't seen hide nor hair of a bomb. And chances are nobody else did. Those newspaper fellers certainly can think things up. They're the ones that started.

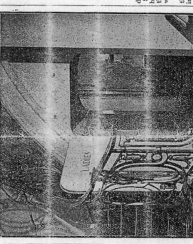

ESCAPES GRATIFY SMUG SAVOYARDS

Prayers For Churchill Feature Holiday Rites

The records will show that within three weeks after war was declared Edward Angly, that intrepid adventurer, moved into the Savoy Hotel. As correspondent for the New York Herald-Tribune, he had raced breathlessly across the ocean to cover a war and with the unerring instinct of all bold and fearless leaders taken cover within as thick as a set of walls as London claims.

The records will not show it, but it is not fanciful to suppose that, for a time at least, he paid the price of loneliness for his initiative. It is not unreasonable, and of course it makes a pretty picture, to think of Angly in his few doors from his own. So meals and off duty breaks were often spent together.

Neville Chamberlain resigned as Prime Minister in that year and a National Government was formed under the leadership of Winston Churchill. Chamberlain died six months later of cancer. London suffered heavy bombing by the Luftwaffe and the high altar of St Paul's Cathedral was destroyed. The RAF fought and won the Battle of Britain in the skies over southern England – the Germans lost 1733 aircraft and the British lost 915.

Three contingencies in Derek's life were to profile his destiny: his world trip; the writing of his book *Time Was Mine*; and, of course, the event of the war. The first two were under his control and, like chemical compounds, once they were mixed with the potential of the third, all three became locked in one providence.

On 27 April 1939, at 20 years of age, slim and attractive Jean Nicol was interviewed for the post of a secretary in the publicity office, in room 205, at the Savoy Hotel, which was just off the Strand in London. The fact that she was the successful applicant for the position added a fourth and final part to Derek Tangye's quest for destiny. If she had not secured that job there would have been no haven of the future established at Minack and no chronicles to lift readers through their lives – in fact, it has to be considered that Derek and Jean would never have met and got married, not unless one ascends to a more towering belief in destiny.

14

In 1919 the British scientist Ernest Rutherford discovered the proton: the tiny gem of an element with a positive charge that, together with other constituents, "balances" out the structure of every kind of known atom. Jean Nicol was born in that same year, on 23 March. And the foregoing statement on the proton might well have been a prophesy on her well "balanced" judgement and personality in mature life. 1919 was also the year of Dame Margot Fonteyn's birth. Lady Astor became the first woman to take her seat in the House of Commons.

Jean Everald Nicol was born, a fine and healthy baby, the first of two sisters, in a nursing home at 69 Oxford Road, Chiswick: close to the river Thames and a stone's throw from Kew Gardens. The nursing home was a little more than a mile, as the crow flies, from Thames Bank Cottage at Mortlake – a comfortable home she would one day swap for a decayed old cottage in a remote and exposed region of Cornwall. On the very day she entered the world, seven-year-old Derek Tangye was living with his mother and father in Cologne, in Germany.

Her delighted parents were Frank Claude Nicol, a rating surveyor and a former captain in the 10th London Regiment, and Dora (née Mackenzie), his wife. Their home was close to the nursing home, at 39 Cambridge Road, Chiswick. From her mother, Jean inherited a steadfast Scottish tenacity. She also possessed a heart that was as forgiving as it was understanding. And as an early statement of her love for mute creatures, from the moment she could crawl she was drawn to animals.

Within two years her parents took her to live in Troon, a small harbour community in Ayrshire, Scotland. It was there that their second daughter Barbara was born. But there came a need to return south, and that was where the two girls grew up, inspired by the love and security of a happy family home.

Like many men who adored their daughters, Frank Nicol tried to teach his just what he had always considered to be the underlying principles of all that was good and decent in a life on earth. He was aware that the society in which he would bring them up set many standards that were not always manageable, given certain circumstances in a real world. He wanted to see them grow up to be happy, with families of their own – married to men who possessed ambition and who were steadfast of mind. Compassion, in his opinion, was a lifeline that could be thrown to the less fortunate souls in life. 'Help them to comprehend their problems and you'll understand your own much better – for when it comes to wretchedness there is no mind immune to its potential.'

Frank Nicol was considerably influenced in such an opinion for he had witnessed the suffering minds of those less fortunate than himself. Even when he was gassed by the enemy on the battlefields of the Great War of 1914–18 he gave thanks for his mercy. He had since watched the building of Sir Edward Lutyens' memorial, the Cenotaph, in Whitehall, just a short distance from Westminster Abbey and, in memory of the fallen of his own regiment, he attended its unveiling.

When Frank Nicol returned to London to work he rented an attractive Edwardian house in St Albans. It was a comfortable home and he fell in love with it. He approached the owner with an offer to purchase the property but was turned down. So he acquired a generous plot of land close by and built a house of his own design, which he affectionately named Bryher Lodge – after a tiny island that was part of the Scilly Isles and where he had taken the family to enjoy a holiday the previous Easter. Bryher Lodge was to be the family home for Jean and Barbara until the day they both got married.

In 1927 it was safe for children to walk the quiet lanes and to roam the countryside footpaths – in that same way, people sometimes left front doors unlocked when absent from their homes. And so it was that, at the ages of eight and six years respectively, Jean and Barbara often took the family dog for a walk on the footpath that skirted St Albans golf course. As children, there was plenty that took their attention and so much to talk about. It was a memorable time that became a dawning for Jean's imagination in her ability to tell stories – a flair she could have used well, together with her love of animals, if she had become a writer of children's stories later in her life – a talent in which she would surely have equalled her husband's success with the *Minack Chronicles*.

She had one particular character whom she favoured and, as they strolled, Barbara would hear about the adventures and the exploits of "Alice who lived in a palace". And sometimes as they sat on the grass, one child telling a story as the other listened intently, the dog would sit with them, attentive also, as though caught up in the story. But with such inventiveness Jean sometimes became a victim of her own imagination; and there were times when she found it difficult, at home or at school, to relate to the absolute truth of a situation. Such was her inspiration and her artistry that she would one day write, in the hand of fiction, a trilogy of "hotel" books, in which she would draw on her experiences at the Savoy Hotel as a backdrop. It was her imagination in the storyline, together with her ability to write, that made each of the books so popular. And, together with her autobiography, *Meet Me at the Savoy*, all four books now have a collector's value.

The two Nicol sisters attended the private Westgate School for five years, where they were boarders. To the headmistress, Miss Webber, all resident girls were something of an extended family. The school was housed to the west of Margate, in Kent, and it had the good fortune to possess a private beach that was used for physical education as well as recreation. High standards were expected of the young ladies and a good education was on offer for a fee that was commensurate with some of the better known private schools of the time. Although Westgate school was distanced from London, the uniforms were purchased from Harrods in Knightsbridge and for Jean Nicol this became an introduction to a fashionable store that would one day play a leading role in her chosen career.

At the school, where they were taught the artistry of Greek dancing and aural culture, both sisters were popular but were almost opposites. Jean did well in the arts, with geography as one of her strongest subjects. Horse riding was another skill in the school curriculum and in this she possessed a natural aptitude, it being a talent she could have considered as a career option. English was also a subject that Jean had no difficulty with – in fact, whilst at Westgate School, she even considered journalism as a possible profession of the future. Barbara was the more athletically inclined with a score of credits in tennis, netball and lacrosse. But Jean suffered no sense of rivalry with Barbara – one girl was never envious of the other. As sisters they had a bond of unspoken love and devotion and, as with Derek and his brothers, their age difference gave them separate friends – which was sometimes inclined to detach them from each other. Whilst at the school they were given the opportunity to travel and they were fortunate to visit some of the European capitals.

In the early 1930s the young ladies of such schools were not necessarily encouraged to be career minded. So they were taught how to become good mothers, how to keep a splendid home and most important, to know how to be a perfect host at a dinner party that might be given in honour of their husband's business colleagues.

Both sisters captured the admiration of their tutors and although one gave Jean a disparaging report – "Jean has no sense of responsibility" – some were quick to witness her skill in her balance of judgement of others.

Many years later, when World War II began, Westgate School was on one of the first lines of defence on the home front – for it was entombed behind metal and concrete tank traps that had been hastily erected along the shoreline, should Hitler decide to invade the southern coastline of England. So the school was vacated and closed, to be instantly requisitioned by the War Department as accommodation for British servicemen who manned the defences.

It is an amusing footnote to the school that many years after the war had finished, Barbara had an occasion to meet a man to whom, in the course of conversation, she spoke of being a former pupil of Westgate School. She discovered that the man had known the building as a serviceman and had been billeted there in the early war years. It became apparent that he had slept in the dormitory that she had once occupied. He told her how he settled down each night on a lumpy straw palliasse on the floor and looked on the wall above his bed space to see a bell-push that had a notice beneath it – "Ring for a mistress"!

After Westgate School, Jean returned home and she attended St Albans High School. It is not known if such a sideways move was for reasons of family economy. Later she enrolled at a local college where she learned the skills of writing in shorthand and typewriting. The typewriter was once considered to be an instrument that somehow gave its young female operator a posture that was appealing to the male eye – there is no such admiration for the modern computer user. There also existed a bearing more seductive in a stenographer who sat upright, with crossed and shapely legs, rapidly writing words in Pitman's shorthand, in a notebook, as she took dictation. And such was an early image of Jean.

For those hopeful of a career in journalism, articles written for newspapers and magazines were a beginning and a valuable source of experience. Jean saw herself as a probationer to the profession as she keenly tapped away at her typewriter keys. Nevertheless, each well constructed article was returned with a rejection slip, praising her work, and telling her to keep trying. But one rejection inspired her. It came in the form of a letter from the editor of a newspaper who wanted to offer her encouragement by saying that she showed promise. She used the letter as a reference and with it she gained employment with the *Daily Mirror*. She was 19 years of age and was without experience in serious matters of the heart – especially in the lives of others. Nevertheless, she was given the opportunity to become an agony aunt, using the pen name of Dorothy Dix. Readers wrote to her seeking advice and direction.

Human emotions are sometimes misinterpreted in their need for understanding and the resultant passions of an unstable mind can create a volatile and disastrous situation in the lives of others. And so it was, in the last year of her teens, Jean Nicol made a brave attempt to make sense of the complicated problems of the many Dorothy Dix readers. The job was difficult in that it required the skill of a psychoanalyst.

One of her morning postbags produced a letter from a former prefect of her old Westgate school – whom she remembered as having something of a caustic tongue. It was plain that the writer was unaware of the true identity of Miss Dorothy Dix. The girl was involved in a love triangle and it was a stereotype of the kind of an association that had occurred countless millions of times in the history of all civilisation – yet there was still no easy answer to such a complication.

Jean's age, and her inexperience in the matters that fell into her lap from the postbag each morning judged her bluntly, and she was unkindly sacked after writing the page for just a few weeks. She had worked for the same newspaper as Derek Tangye and in the same building – and in those few weeks their paths had not crossed once. She had been dismissed by an editor who would soon be instrumental in the clearing of Derek's desk – before taking his world trip, of course.

Derek Tangye was well publicised in the writing of his own column – and Jean always remembered how she had walked out of the *Daily Mirror* offices, on her last day of employment, to be confronted by a large head and shoulders picture of him as he smiled down at her from the side of a bus. It was a display of publicity that blazed his name and his vinegary viewpoint column all over London. For a brief moment Jean Nicol almost resented him – but that was only because his apparent success was a representation of the same employer who was responsible for the misery that she felt at that particular moment.

On 27 April 1939, just over four months before the outbreak of war, Jean Nicol walked down the Strand during the morning rush of commuters. She was on her way to start a new job at the Savoy Hotel. She had been interviewed there the previous week, in room 205, for the junior position of a secretary to the publicity manager's assistant. Now, it was a Monday morning and she hurried across the busy road in front of Woolworth's – she was feeling a little nervous as she anticipated her new job. It was just five weeks since she had celebrated her twentieth birthday and, on this morning in particular, she had taken good care with her make-up. As she stepped onto the pavement once again she admired her trim figure as it was reflected in a shop window. She was dressed in a smart navy-blue suit that was contrasted with a white blouse. It pleased her that she had been the successful applicant and her intuition was already telling her that, in this position, she may well have found her niche.

When she entered room 205, her usual manner did not suggest self-reliance and an engaging disposition and therefore this was not immediately recognised by her new employer. But on that day it was likely that the very first letter of the first word of the poem *The Spirits of Minack* was being symbolically written on a wind that was already blowing over a distant meadow on a Cornish clifftop.

Jean's boss was a sporting type with the name of John Hannay. He, in his turn, was an assistant to the Publicity Manager, Mr Tritton. Shortly after beginning work on that first day she was on her knees scanning the pages of daily newspapers that were spread out on the office floor, searching for the tiniest nuggets in print that could be used, in some way, for the publicity of the hotel. The Savoy Hotel was to introduce her to the merits of independence through the practice of self-sufficiency; every coulomb of electricity the building used in its emergency supply was generated from its own power station, and wells that had been sunk deep into the underground aquifers gave up an ample supply of pure and clean water.

After spending four of the most interesting months of her life in room 205, Jean Nicol knew she did not want to work anywhere else – the Savoy Hotel was indeed a good employer. The vibrant energy that was contained therein was of its own excitement and life never stood still. The atmosphere was often one of exaltation and then calamitous sudden drama. There was laughter, and happiness, music and dancing. Delectable and exotic foods were almost beyond the capability of the imagination, created by some of the world's best chefs – who magically produced culinary surprises from the basic wartime ration of food supplies. There came through the swing doors of the Savoy Hotel the most famous of faces in the world of entertainment and leading politicians of prominent nations. To be a waiter, hall porter, barman, or chambermaid in that particular hotel was to be engaged in a profession of its own interpretation – not a trade. Such was the level of expertise that was called for that any employee, on any level, whose commitment failed to show such an educated attitude was not invited to stay longer than the trial period of their employment.

In the uncertain days, after the war had begun, there were many executive "oval table" meetings that were intended to ascertain the future of the hotel for the duration. After one such meeting the publicity manager's assistant, John Hannay, informed Jean that the outlook for the Savoy Hotel would be bleak as there would be no guests arriving from abroad – in particular the United States. He suggested that she should take a week's holiday while she had the opportunity and while final decisions were being made. So she took the night train from Waterloo to Newton Abbot, in Devon, and stayed in a farmhouse – a place of a previous family holiday. At 11 am the following Sunday she listened to the radio with the farmer and his family, as Prime Minister Neville Chamberlain announced over the airwaves that Britain was at war with Germany. They all stood up in a moment's silence – and then, spontaneously and patriotically, they held hands and sang the national anthem.

At that moment in time, Derek Tangye, who had returned from a world trip a matter of months earlier, was in Falmouth settling into his first whole day as a private soldier in the Duke of Cornwall's Light Infantry.

After the prime minister's wireless address, Jean walked to the local telephone box which was perched on top of a nearby hill, and from there she sent a telegram to her employer seeking some kind of direction. She received a reply by return of post informing her that John Hannay expected to be called up for military service and that would mean she would have no one to work for, as the publicity department would have to run on a skeleton level of staffing. Conclusively – there was no longer a job there for her!

After just two uncertain months of the war had passed, the Publicity Manager, Mr Tritton, telephoned her at her St Albans home and offered her John Hannay's post, as he had, indeed, been called up – and there was a need to retain an assistant to the publicity manager. She returned to a Savoy Hotel, which gave her a welcome like that of a star guest. When Mr Tritton was eventually to leave his post as the Publicity Manager, it was to join the Public Relations Department at the War Office and his place was taken by Jean Lorimer, who had previously been writing for the *Sunday Dispatch*. Although Jean was competent in her work at the Savoy Hotel, Fleet Street never lost its pulling ability for her and she finally decided to return to her first love of journalism.

Mr Miles Thornewill was a director of the hotel group. He was slim with an appearance that was elegant as well as aristocratic. When he summoned Jean Nicol to his office, she feared that he considered she was falling somewhat short in the performance of her duties and he was going to diplomatically suggest that she should resign her post. She strode the long corridors of the hotel with a little apprehension, using the stairway rather than the lift because the attendant was always chatty – and on this occasion she felt reluctant to be engaged in his small talk.

Miles Thornewill's polite greeting was deceptive to her – but then he had always been courteous in his manner, no matter what the occasion. And, as she sat humbly facing him across his desk, she was ready to explain herself in whatever way was required. Every syllable he uttered was an antithesis of those she had carried there inside her head. He informed her that Miss Jean Lorimer had decided to return to Fleet Street and that she (Jean Nicol) would be the new Publicity Manager with, of course, an appropriate increase in her salary.

It mattered not to Jean Nicol that her remuneration was not on a parity with that of her predecessor, for it seemed to her there were more important things to consider now. As the post meant being constantly on call she was given an elegant suite in the hotel and she dined in the main restaurant, choosing from the guest menu. And so, in 1940, at the age of 21, Jean Nicol was on the threshold of becoming one of the greatest purveyors of publicity the Savoy Hotel was to know. She was already aware of the tact and the fine line of discretion that her work would call for. And it was not long before she began to be unofficially summoned in the role of a peacemaker, in a dispute between the heads of departments who intimidated each other, often with the use of threats.

Vic Gower retired from the Savoy Hotel in the 1990s after giving 50 years of faithful service there. For most of that time he worked in the American Bar, but when he started he was a 16-year-old pageboy. Along with the other pageboys he remembers Jean Nicol as being more beautiful than any of the legendary goddesses of the Hollywood silver screen who had often stayed at the Savoy. But, in her own infinite beauty through others' eyes, Jean was never to develop the mega-ego of some of those actresses. She was, nevertheless, often obliged to deal with their petty ways, and in this she succeeded with well meaning consideration. Vic Gower is keen to support the claim that Jean Nicol was, indeed, a legend in her own time. As a part of her job, she made the arrangements to receive sovereigns and world leaders at the Savoy and she was sometimes invited to dine with them. Her reputation went before her and she enhanced the hotel's standing on far continents. Many distinguished visitors to London became intent on staying there in order to meet her. She endured more late nights than she cared for and, together with her guests, she braved the dangers of the Luftwaffe bombing raids after dark, as people danced to the band of Carroll Gibbons and the Savoy Orpheans in a live broadcast, on the BBC light entertainment airwaves. Such transmissions from London became a morale booster to listeners in all parts of the country, as people, young and old, huddled beneath blankets in small Anderson shelters in the back garden or Morrison iron table shelters in the living room, while an air raid was in progress.

It was inherent in her job, especially in wartime, that the Savoy Hotel should demand, and succeed in getting, much of her waking time. But occasionally she was able to meet with her sister Barbara who worked as a secretary just a short distance away, in the office of the forces entertainment organisation ENSA in Drury Lane; and over coffee in a nearby restaurant they were able to catch up on family matters and gossip. At weekends, when time allowed, they had the occasional Sunday together helping the WVS, by driving a mobile canteen around the outskirts of the family home town of St Albans. Their voluntary task was to supply refreshments to servicemen who manned anti-aircraft guns or who performed other essential duties. On one particular Christmas day, men on the sites they visited were insistent that the two attractive young women should dine with them in their spartan mess huts. They were reluctant but did not want to offend their hosts; and by the time they arrived home for their family Christmas dinner they had already consumed two complete festive meals.

The war years brought a great change in clientele for the Savoy Hotel – although world-famous star entertainers like Danny Kaye, Gregory Peck, Tyrone Power, Errol Flynn, Mae West, Carol Landis, Gertrude Lawrence and a host of others still came, drawn to its luxurious suites and glamorous lifestyle that, somehow, managed to survive in spite of the Luftwaffe's intensive bombing raids. It speaks well of those entertainers that they would come to Britain and, along with British actors and actresses, risk their lives to help keep the West End theatres open and alive.

While remaining a world-class hotel, the Savoy also became a frenzied and loquacious nerve-centre of dialogue in news gathering and it became a place of mechanised processing of words for the media. *Time* magazine was represented and all other such major US publications and newspapers. Many of the rooms were occupied as work stations by celebrated and distinguished names in American journalism. Radio networks such as the NBC set up a base there, enabling the American broadcaster and war correspondent Ed Murrow to transmit his historic descriptions live to listeners coast to coast in the United States while much of London was being destroyed around him by German bombs. Throughout the war Titch's Bar remained a news-gathering "market place" within the hotel where journalists met to exchange stories of their own "near misses" and to tap into the grapevine.

The Savoy Hotel was hit by high explosive bombs twice in one night. On another occasion the whole of the riverside front was blown out by an enormous aerial mine that descended by parachute and was caught in the branches of a nearby tree – it swung defiantly in its harness for a moment and then exploded. For the first time since the hotel had been built in 1889, as the first completely fire-proofed building in the world, it was under the threat of fire that came from the sky and not from within. In one night, as many of the buildings in the centre of London burned, scores of incendiary bombs had to be cleared from the roof of the hotel to prevent it too from catching fire – but not once, throughout the whole of the war, did the Savoy close its doors!

Jean Nicol not only coped with the often frenzied demands of her own work and was pursued, also, by those in the entertainment business who were constantly in need of her advice – and it seemed that many of the journalists often sought her as an unpaid assistant. All who knew her, in those most prime of her times, were impressed with her ability to converse with them on just about any subject they cared to choose. When the great seagoing liners disembarked VIPs at Southampton's Ocean Terminal, arrangements were made to transport them to London, where Publicity Manager Jean Nicol was always available in the front hall of the Savoy Hotel to greet them on their arrival and to advise them – sometimes over a drink in the American Bar at 1 am – after an exhausting day.

The huge canopied concourse that linked the Savoy Hotel with the Strand was heavily sandbagged to protect the vast plateglass front, with its swing doors, from bomb blast. At night, as with the rest of the country, the streets of London were plunged into darkness. The "blackout" was an important measure of Britain's defence, to prevent German night-flying bombers from identifying potential targets. Gone were the glittering lights that encircled Piccadilly Circus and those that illuminated the fronts of West End theatres and bars. In keeping with all other buildings the Savoy Hotel installed heavy blackout curtains in all its rooms, to prevent the tiniest chink of light from showing through; even the glass in the swing doors was coated with a thick blue paint.

Jean Nicol, in her own special task, probably played a role for the Savoy group of hotels that was more cardinal even than that of Hugh Wontner, who became the general manager and then a director. But time, it seems, has stolen much of her memory there, for there are but a few members of the staff today who know of her name. Nevertheless, in the researching of this book she has been kissed as a modern sleeping beauty and stirred from her slumber; for her memory is once again celebrated within the majestic walls of that palace, which continues today as the Savoy Hotel. A dark-framed whole plate-sized photograph, taken of Jean Nicol and her husband Derek soon after they were married, was presented in her memory to the Savoy Hotel publicity office by this author, and there she will remain until the building starts to crumble or to the end of eternity – whichever should happen first. Unfortunately, the wall that holds the picture is not the same one that she used for such a display in room 205, which was formerly her office, and is now a kitchen where light meals are prepared for room service – the publicity office has been moved to the other side of the building.

Without a doubt, Jean Nicol had intelligence, wit and beauty. No man was at a loss for words in her company because she possessed knowledge enough to converse on whatever his chosen theme or thesis. Her very personality was such that it flirted mildly with the opposite gender and she, quite innocently, had a manner that flattered the average man to feel that she found him good to know. Such were the attributes of her personality and her appearance that she need never be short of acceptable suitors in her life – but such an active life at the Savoy Hotel limited her time for romance.

Danny Kaye fell for her and he wined and dined her without publicity (something that would be impossible to keep from the roving eye of today's tabloids). She admired and respected him, but she knew he was not free to woo her deeply and, despite their underlying emotions that sought to immerse them in a more sincere and heartfelt involvement, they struggled in a friendship that was destined to be seen as one that was simply platonic. On and off the stage of the London Palladium, Danny Kaye was always known to be a clown, just as he was on Broadway. But he was a clown with a lonely heart. In the company of others he was always the lovable fool and people warmed to him.

He seemed emotionally fearless and he made them laugh constantly. Unable to have Jean for his own, Danny reconciled his feelings for her as being those for a surrogate lover. She often accompanied him in his private life and, in doing so, she was able to lift the mask of foolery from his face to discover what lay behind it. He explained to her how, as a kid, he was popular at parties because he made the rest of the gang laugh. But, came the end of the party, the other boys got the girls and he went home alone – and such is the loneliness that still lives today within the heart of many a court jester.

As a popular person, in her own young social life, Jean had never known the restrictions of emotional hangups. Nevertheless, she understood the courage it had taken for him to tell her that, all his life, he had been a sentimental fool – which hindered his potential to show that he was also a lovable one. He risked his life by coming to Britain and performing through the terrible air raids – and each time, in his quest to see her just one more time, he was even more popular with London audiences than with those in New York. When he became less celebrated in the USA he made a commitment to UNICEF and he entertained unfortunate children in underdeveloped countries – clowns can easily climb over the barrier of any language by the use of their foolery – and he possessed an amazing ability to reach children at their own level of humour.

When he played opposite Gertrude Lawrence in *Lady in the Dark*, on Broadway, he constantly sought news of Jean, knowing Gertrude to be a dear friend who was in constant touch. Jean and Danny never met again after she took up her life in Minack. But in 1983 she was concerned when she learned he had undergone quadruple bypass surgery in the United States – from which he never truly recovered. He died in 1987, at the age of 74 years, of hepatitis and internal bleeding. He had been given a transfusion of contaminated blood after the operation. Jean never knew of his passing; for she had died just one year earlier.

15

Craig Thompson was the assistant chief of the *New York Times* bureau whose room at the Savoy Hotel was his workstation also. He was lanky, dark-haired and wore a Ronald Coleman moustache. His persona was that of a Hollywood movie actor and he was an expressively home-loving American who missed momma's home-made apple pie. It did not take him long to fall for Jean. His appeal for her was that he was more humble in his approach and attitude – more than the average high-flying New Yorker she had encountered in the newspaper profession hitherto. Their romance was not a deep relationship; nevertheless she took him home to St Albans to stay some weekends, where he got to know her mother and father. Sisters sometimes compared boyfriends and she wondered just what Barbara's opinion of him would be.

Harold Keeble was the features editor for the *Daily Express*. He too fell deeply for Jean and was hopeful that one day he would ask her father for her hand in marriage. He considered himself to have a fair chance against the pool of competition and he drove her to Bishop's Stortford to meet his own mother.

Bill White was fair with a prematurely receding hairline and he wore the Glenn Miller rimless glasses that were popular with Americans of that era. He was, nevertheless, a handsome man with features resembling Tangye's and with a similar physique. When Jean first knew him, he was with the Associated Press, but later he joined the *New York Herald Tribune* before becoming a bureau chief for *Time* magazine: all three organisations were based at the Savoy Hotel. Home for Bill was in Denver, Colorado. With an air of providence about his life, he was likened to the boy who lived in the attractive house where roses clung to a white picket fence on a tree-lined avenue. His manner was that of a young man whom any parent would be happy to have as a son-in-law.

Bill was attentive and kind to Jean and she met him as an alternative regular boyfriend – for she was dating Derek Tangye at the same time. The two men were both earnest contenders and when they eventually knew of each other, they became locked in rivalry. Bill White proposed to Jean, but she was uncertain and she turned him down. She felt he was a capable and very independent person and she wondered whether he *really* needed her. When she took him home at weekends he played golf with her father and helped her mother to wash the Sunday dinner dishes. He was a good conversationalist. He had ambition and a clear idea of where he was going. Frank and Dora Nicol were hopeful they would one day welcome him into their family.

The *Savoy Standard* was born of an idea Jean Nicol had about producing a newspaper that was exclusive to the Savoy Hotel. It was of the same format as the London *Evening Standard*. The first edition became available in the front hall on Thursday, 27 November 1941. The editor was listed as Jean Nicol, with associate editors Robert P. Post, Joseph Evans, William W. White (Derek Tangye's rival, Bill), James MacDonald and Craig Thompson (a former boyfriend), and there were numerous contributors. Every article was light-hearted or humorous – including letters to the editor – and the paper reflected the need for mindful escapism at a time when death fell every day from the skies and survival was uncertain.

As an archive document, it is buried treasure rediscovered and it conveys an objective view of a segment of civilian life in wartime Britain. It reveals the unprecedented status of the Savoy Hotel in those years and the important role it came to play in the war. The first edition contains a little story that illustrates the shortage of one of the most basic of foods in wartime – the humble fresh egg. Two resident pressmen vied for a simple boiled egg for their breakfast after they had both discovered there was only one available. The man who had successfully charmed the waiter proceeded to eat it in front of his companion – the other man suggested to the waiter, in earnest, that he should return to the kitchen immediately and appeal to the chef on his behalf, for he craved what was only available to his colleague. The story has no punchline but it effectively demonstrates the mark of austerity that existed and the perverse attitudes that can dwell between friends at such a time. This was just one of many unimportant little stories that almost belied the luxuriant lifestyle that was still apparently available at the Savoy Hotel. In contrast to that story of extreme lack, there did exist, in fact, a most delectable menu and this was largely due to the almost unrivalled skills of the head chef and his team.

Now destiny led Captain Derek Tangye of the Intelligence Corps, smartly dressed in his khaki uniform and with a highly polished Sam Brown belt strapped diagonally across his chest, to push the revolving doors of the Savoy Hotel and to enter the front hall. He was followed by his long-time friend Ronald Hyde, who was the news editor of the *Evening Standard*. It was a cold January day in1941.

The Publicity Manager, Jean Nicol, had developed a keen sense of awareness about new arrivals as a part of her job. She had a penchant to remember faces and as a result she instantly recognised the young officer's face as being the one that had looked down at her from an advertisement on the side of a bus, on the day she had lost her job as Dorothy Dix with the *Daily Mirror*.

Ronald Hyde had already made an acquaintance with Jean Nicol on another occasion and he introduced Derek Tangye to her. Derek was quick to offer her a polite 'How-do-you-do' and then he informed her, 'I've been wanting to meet you – I've just written a book called *Time Was Mine* and I wondered if you would display it on the Savoy bookstall?'

His words were breathless. Both Jean and Ronald excused the impulsive manner of his request with a polite and gentle laugh. Then Ronald Hyde led them into the Savoy Grill as his guests for lunch – his intention was one of matchmaking; Derek's intention was one of publicity to promote his book.

Now, as Derek sat at the luncheon table, he had time to observe Jean Nicol more closely. He *had* noticed her on a previous occasion when he had dined at the Savoy and they had communicated with a momentary impersonal glance across a crowded restaurant. He had felt an instant awareness of her. She, on the other hand, had become used to men who might sneak an admiring glance in her direction – and could not recall the event. Ronald Hyde was mindful of his friend's interest in Jean Nicol, for Derek had already confided in him. That luncheon was to remain the most memorable of meals in the lives of all three present.

When Derek began to date Jean on a regular basis, he was not aware that she intended to continue to see Bill White, and the situation became somewhat bizarre. Her mother and father and her sister Barbara were all aware of her divided affections for both men. Her parents had, by then, read *Time Was Mine* and were negatively impressed with the content of some of the pages. Derek's purported sexual encounters with the young South Sea Island girls alarmed Frank and Dora Nicol – especially the story about the girl who appeared to have been below the age of consent. Jean's father could only see Derek with the status of an island beachcomber who would bum a living for the rest of his life. Barbara was more sympathetic, for she was not convinced the deeds had actually taken place. She also better understood some of the ways of her own generation, who sought to rid themselves of the influence of staid Victorian literature – and if Derek Tangye was, in fact, using the facility of writer's licence to sensationalise his experiences to further the promotion of the book, then, for many readers, it was a step in the right direction towards the emancipation of the arts.

After the publication of the book, Derek's name was hardly to be mentioned in the Nicol household and Jean was encouraged to take Bill White home more frequently. Talk of an engagement to the American was often to be prompted by her parents as a more positive expression for a secure future. Secretly, Jean was seeing Derek more frequently than even Barbara knew.

Although Derek Tangye held the rank of a captain in the Intelligence Corps he knew his commission was only a wartime one and, if he survived the war, he would not be invited to continue as an officer in a peacetime army. So the permanency he now found in his life was but a shallow one. Debts still remained, especially at the Savoy Hotel – this, he excused himself, was not due to poor management but to the burden of his army mess fees. With no money, he could not promise Jean Nicol anything of a future, but if he hesitated further he stood to lose her to his adversary. Jean was painfully aware that she too had an important decision to make. Should she choose a life that would be regulated by convention as Mrs White? Or should she wake up each morning as Mrs Tangye, uncertain of what the coming years might bring? There was no yardstick to guide her in her judgement – bar that of a woman's intuition.

Derek and Bill had once been good buddies, but their rivalry had got in the way and had spoiled their friendship. In the summer of 1941 Derek was able to get permission from the War Office to live in Richmond, where he took on the rental of a Regency dwelling called Cholmondely House that commanded a picturesque view of the river Thames. It had pale blue railings and a display of potted geraniums, and the house became affectionately known as 'Chummy'. The rent was more than Derek could comfortably afford, and he overcame that problem by subletting two of the rooms. One was, most surprisingly, to Bill White and the other to another American journalist, Joe Paris. But the tangled emotions of rivalry for the love of the same maiden caused Bill White to pull out of the deal. This created an embarrassing gap that tilted the financial balance.

When Derek wrote of this incident in the *Minack Chronicles* he never explained the reason behind it. He was critical of Bill White in his words, claiming that he was irresponsible and never paid his rent. Ronald Hyde was aware of the animosity between the two men, and he stepped in to breach the financial gap by taking the room for himself.

In the winter of 1942, Derek proposed marriage to Jean. He had waited for over an hour for her in a pub on the Strand, not far from the Savoy Hotel, called the Coalhole. He had decided to seize his chance because Jean had agreed to call it off with Bill White, saying there would be no further relationship between them. Now, as he waited with the engagement ring already in his pocket, Derek was unsure. Had she not told Bill of her decision? Worse still – had she changed her mind? Derek drank for reassurance and ordered another vodka. Suddenly the door opened and he braced himself for the icy blast that came in with each new arrival. As Jean appeared in the doorway he felt suddenly warmed – but still unsure of himself. She smiled at him, radiantly, and she apologised to him. She gave him a peck on the cheek and a reason for her lateness but he was not listening to her words.

'Will you marry me?' he suddenly asked her, in a manner that had the same rush of urgency as in the front hall of the Savoy Hotel, when he had asked her to display his book *Time Was Mine*.

Her answer was quick and spontaneous – almost without consideration. 'Yes.' And although she was to have a lifetime of loving him, she was later to write in her book *Meet Me at the Savoy* that she had never understood exactly why she had agreed so readily to his sudden proposal, because, until that moment, she had been unable to feel absolutely comfortable about the prospect.

The following day Jean telephoned her sister Barbara in her Drury Lane office. 'I've got engaged,' she told her.

'Oh, that's wonderful news,' Barbara replied with delight. 'Bill is such a lovely fellow – I know you'll be very happy.'

Jean hesitated; her voice dropped a little in its tone.

'It's Derek I've got engaged to – not Bill. I've just rung home and broken the news – Mummy and Daddy aren't very happy about it!'

Derek Tangye's next production was a book called *Went The Day Well*. It was a compilation of contributions, from other writers, as a tribute to men and women who had died in World War II. The book was published in 1942 and the title came from an anonymous poem that he read in a visitor's book somewhere. He started almost immediately to interview people, collect material and chomp his way through mountains of fodder in preparation for yet another book to be called *One King*. That was to be a survey of the colonies and the dominions of the British Empire.

Derek Tangye showed a great dedication in the writing of his books and this should have been an indication, to himself as well as to others, of his way forward for the future. He was fortunate to have been able to devote so much of his time to this role in his life when he had military duties to fulfil at the same time.

He was known in those days at the Savoy Hotel as an arrogant man who, it seemed, was only socially malleable at times of his own choosing. Whereas barmen, waiters, hall porters, and the like were known to hotel management and guests by their first names, Captain Tangye would coldly refer to them by their surnames – a practice for which Jean constantly admonished him. So often, when he called to see her, she was in demand due to her work and she might be expected to have a meal in the Savoy Grill with a male companion in the course of her duties, to discuss hotel business. At such times Derek sat alone on a high stool in the American Bar drinking more vodka than was good for him and, because of his social demeanour, he was never to get the benefit of a sympathetic ear in conversation with any of the bartenders. When Jean Nicol told her boss, director Miles Thornewill, of her impending marriage, he questioned her, in an expression of disapproval, 'To Captain Tangye?'

The drinking continued in an unhealthy vein and it influenced Derek's attitude towards many of whom he should have been more considerate. The Managing Director of the Savoy Hotel, Hugh Wontner, finally approached him and asked of him that he should stop using the facilities of the hotel, as people were now talking about him. But he was obstinate and he continued to drink there – only now he allowed himself to be Derek Tangye once more, no longer conceited in his need to be recognised as an army captain. As such, he worked at becoming more amiable. He drank a little less and made a note of the bartenders' given names.

Individualists have their own way of dealing with their problems and this is often in a practice that is rarely understood by others. When they possess an inner conflict of their feelings they are reluctant to communicate this to others – this sometimes makes them appear aloof and secretive. Their apparent arrogance is an essential part of the machinery of their defence and, while their words can be quite thrusting, they sometimes have to exercise a great effort to overcome a shyness that dwells uncomfortably within them. Jean's ability to understand others gave her just such a perception of her fiancé and she resolved to stand by him – it was her comprehension that he was, and always would be, in need of her.

On the eve of her wedding, Jean Nicol was required, in her duties as Publicity Manager, to attend a function in the Savoy Ballroom that continued till past midnight. So when her sister Barbara arrived at her suite the following morning, to help her to prepare for her marriage that day, she discovered her in bed and still asleep. A breakfast of black coffee and toast was hurriedly brought to her room. And, with the help of Mrs Butler the head housekeeper, Jean slid into a bridal gown that had been created for her by Norman Hartnell, and her veiled tiara was attractively arranged on her head. As many of the staff gathered to wish the bride every happiness, Jean was chauffeured, with her sister in

108

attendance, to Richmond Church. The fact that the ceremony was not to be held in her own parish church of St Albans was a reflection of the feeling that remained entrenched within her parents.

16

Jean clung lovingly to her father's arm, thankful that he had agreed to give her away in a marriage to a man whom he did not want as a son-in-law. It was midday on Saturday 20 February 1943, when Frank Nicol led his daughter into the little chapel that was an annexe of Richmond Church. Derek waited, tall and smartly dressed in the uniform of an army captain. He stood proudly before the altar with his eldest brother Colin, who was the best man – brother Nigel looked on. The Reverend Harold Gray waited quietly by in anticipation of performing the ceremony. It was a small service with only family in attendance – apart from Ronald Hyde, who had been appointed as an usher. A party of close friends waited at Cholmondely House, with a wedding feast already prepared – Bill White was not among them. Danny Kaye sent the couple his best wishes and, regardless of the romantic relationship that Danny and Jean had once enjoyed, Derek was proud of their former association – for it confirmed to him that his bride was indeed a beautiful young woman, who was desired by matinee idols who had the choice of the world's most glamorous women.

For professional reasons Jean continued to be called by her maiden name at the Savoy Hotel. The marriage took place just over one week before Derek's thirty-first birthday and a little more than four weeks before Jean's twenty-fourth birthday. From hereon, in the reading of this book, Jean Nicol Tangye, as she was to become known, will be referred to as Jeannie, for it was circa February 1943 that Derek showed his tender affection for her by extending her first name as such.

After a happy reception that was in no way marred in its celebration by the reservations of her parents, Jeannie changed into a smart going away costume and Derek swapped his khaki uniform for the comfort of civilian clothes. A friend's car, appropriately decorated, took them on an undignified journey to Victoria railway station and, after a short journey, the couple stepped from a carriage of a Southern Electric train onto a platform that led them through the ticket collector's barrier and on to the concourse of Brighton railway station.

They stayed at the Royal Crescent Hotel on the seafront where, unfortunately, the sea view was obstructed by the presence of defence barriers and heavy guns that took possession of more of the promenade than the eye could see. Concrete blocks and anti-invasion tank traps, made of strong metal poles, looked like a hideous construction in surreal sculpture that stretched to infinity along the shoreline. But love became suddenly blind to the presence of war and all their dreams were of a future in a world that yearned to wallow in love and a heavenly peace.

In the interview for radio that Derek Tangye gave the author in May 1992, he spoke with fond remembrance of that honeymoon:

And then we spent our honeymoon in Sussex, in Brighton, and we used to go to a pub – I think it was called the Cricketers. A very famous publican kept it, called Pitt – Mr Pitt. We had another character there and we used to drink with him; he was a retired clown called Bimbo – there was a carnation always in his buttonhole. And then I remember – I can see it now as I am sitting here [points to the sill of the window beside the front door inside Dorminack cottage]; there's a little jug over there, which we bought in The Lanes, and it has always been known as the "honeymoon jug". So I have great memories of Sussex – yes I do.

In June, just four months after the wedding, Jean's sister Barbara left for Cairo. She was one of 12 young British stenographers who were chosen by ENSA to work as part

111

of the forces entertainment group in the Middle East, for a term of one year. It was one of the conditions that none of the girls was married or engaged to be married. But Barbara *was* engaged. Her fiancé was in the army and fighting in the desert, in the middle east – and she was keen to be closer to him by serving her country abroad. So she took her engagement ring off her finger and hid it close to her heart.

One of her first tasks in Egypt was to accompany Dame Lillian Braithwaite, who had just finished performing in the classic play *Arsenic and Old Lace* at the Savoy Theatre, and who had consented to entertain the British fighting forces overseas. Almost as a miracle, Barbara's fiancé was later posted to Cairo and they were married in Cairo Cathedral. The wedding changed Barbara's status and she was able to remain in Egypt with her husband for the duration of the war years. And when Jeannie finally welcomed her sister Barbara home in 1946, she did so as a proud aunt.

Cholmondley House had become well established as Derek and Jeannie's marital home. It was also a meeting place for journalists and writers. It was at "chummy house" that the Tangyes were eventually to hear the patter of tiny feet around them. As a ginger kitten with marmalade stripes and white paws, Monty was destined to become a fully grown cat to be celebrated by the readers of the *Minack Chronicles* – he was awarded the honour of his name in a celebration of Field-Marshall Montgomery – the British victor at El Alamein. And he was to become the forerunner of a series of cats who played a continuing role in the life ahead at Minack – each one a star of the chronicles in its own right.

Derek and Jeannie were given notice to quit Cholmondely House and, still remaining close to the river Thames, they moved to Thames Bank Cottage at Mortlake, which gave a grandstand view of the finishing line for the Oxford and Cambridge boat race. In wartime Great Britain people looked to anything that could be celebrated, just as an excuse to throw a party. It mattered not which contender won the race – Oxford or Cambridge – and the revelry at Mortlake continued well into the night.

A year later, in 1944, Derek's father died in Richmond Hospital, just before the book *One King* was published. Lt Col R.T.G. Tangye was cremated without fuss and in the absence of traditional military honours, as was his wish, and his ashes were committed to a small wooden casket. It fell to Derek's brother Nigel to carry his father's remains to his beloved home of Glendorgal, in Cornwall. Nigel managed to get an extra ration of petrol for his car and he set out on the journey from London to the south-west coast with the casket placed securely on the back seat. It was a strange and lonely experience for Nigel as he drove the long journey. When he started out he struggled to relate to the contents of the casket as being the father who had been so kind and caring and whom he had loved so very much. At first he viewed the remaining ashes as being no different to those that his father had often knocked out of the bowl of his briar smoking pipe. But as the journey progressed he felt more strongly that his father was spiritually with him. It was almost as if he was sitting in the passenger seat, as he drove the car, and talking about the view on the far side of the windscreen. And he thought of all the good in his father's life, knowing so many people had benefited from his thoughtfulness – Nigel, himself, had learned how to reflect his kindness.

When the car arrived in Cornwall Nigel made a brief visit to Glendorgal, then he carried the casket and scattered the ashes over a small plateau on a clifftop some 20 feet above the sea. It was a place of coarse green grass where his father had often sat and looked out over the small bay towards his home. In the moment he tipped the casket and the contents tumbled out Nigel was filled with deep emotion. There was no breeze and the ashes fell to the ground just where he had scattered them. It was a lonely experience, with no ceremony – just as his father had wished.

Derek Tangye seems to have added an element of intrigue to his wartime role in the confounding world of MI5. In reality, as a captain in the Intelligence Corps and also as a regional liaison officer in MI5, his job was very routine and low key. His writing of that period in his life had used the imaginative approach of a spy thriller writer. He ceased to be attached to MI5 the day before he proceeded on release leave on 3 November 1945. (He was later to write in the *Minack Chronicles* of his own personal involvement with British spies who were later to become traitors, inferring he had remained as a member of MI5 well into the post-war years.) And on 29 December 1945, the day he was released from military service, he was granted the honorary rank of Captain – a title he could have used throughout the rest of his civilian life, but chose not to do.

On 2 September 1945 victory over Japan was celebrated, marking the end of World War II. Prior to that date, on 6 August, the atomic bomb was used for the first time, laying four square miles of Hiroshima to waste and killing 50,000 people. Three days later a second bomb was dropped on Nagasaki. Previously, both targets had not been too far from Derek Tangye's Japanese port of exit, where he had embarked for Korea during his world trip. The people there had been very kind and hospitable to him.

Great Britain was an austere place to live in at the end of a war that had brought about an economic crisis. On 26 July there had been a General Election with the Labour Party romping home, and Prime Minister Clement Attlee formed a government. The cabinet had the unenviable task of creating work for the millions of servicemen who were now returning home from war to civvy street – to pick up a way of life they had been snatched from six years earlier and to settle down to a style of living they had almost forgotten. They had wives and children, some of whom had not seen them for more than half a decade. Many children were unable to recognise their fathers.

Others had fathers who would never return and the family did not have a body over which to mourn. Derek Tangye's second book, *Went The Day Well*, was about many such people who gave their lives in human sacrifice for the freedom of others. Half a century on – how obscure the trail of human memory has become, when time has veiled all such purpose in the minds of many in following generations who have no recollection and care less that the act of dying in that war has allowed them to have a life today – and every soul who perished in that war has qualified to be remembered as a hero!

In 1946 the Labour Government went ahead with its plans to nationalise every industry it could lay its hands on – including the Bank of England. It was not a good time for a speculator with a sack of peanuts and a market stall to have an idea of becoming another F.W. Woolworth. But on the American leg of his pre-war world travels Derek Tangye had witnessed the successful operation of a chain of "takeaway" food shops. He was intrigued by such an idea and he had tucked it at the back of his mind as a sound business prospect for the future.

Back in civilian life he had little money – having always been a spender and not an accumulator. The gratuity he received on his discharge from the army was insufficient for his capital needs, and anyway, unlike his brother Colin, he was not very good at balancing his income with his expenditure. He wrote and sold some articles to national newspapers and the meagre earnings they returned encouraged him in his enthusiasm to take a chance and put the American "takeaway" idea to work.

There were actually two business conceptions that had proved very successful in the United States. But those who bravely tried them out in post-war Britain failed because they tried selling their wares to potential buyers in an austere society where the average householder still had to put a "couple of bob" away in a tin each week for a few days' holiday at the seaside. One idea was that of the launderette, the first of which opened in Bayswater in May 1949. The British housewife had only ever had the demeaning option of slaving over a family wash by boiling it for hours in a copper and rubbing it almost threadbare by hand. Never having owned a washing machine, she was suspicious of its claim to wash each garment clean. As a result, many who ventured into the launderette business found themselves with rows of idle washing machines that were later to be claimed by the County Court bailiff as a part payment for debts. Such was the fate also of some of the early food "takeaway" ventures (the Tangye shop was only the second in the land).

The middle and upper middle classes were not yet accustomed to calling at a shop on the High Street and carrying a cooked meal home in a paper carrier bag with string handles – only the working class, and a few of the hard-pressed middle class, would visit the fish and chip shop or carry a dish of hot pease pudding home.

Derek Tangye had a grand opening for his high-class cuisine shop in Vicarage Road, Kingston on Thames, which he called The Larder – a plain and simple name that humbled the quality of the business he had established. He had brought table d' hôte in a paper bag to the people. He provided high-class food for those who were willing to pay that much more. Two chefs, one French and the other Portuguese, dressed in starched white outfits, worked in a kitchen that was partially on view to the public, while a smartly dressed young lady, who had been appointed as the manageress, served the customers. Derek stood by, flamboyant, wearing a white dinner jacket with the point of a silk handkerchief hanging from his top pocket, a colourful bow tie and brown leather shoes. As he greeted his customers he saw himself in the role of a public relations figurehead who would, almost overnight, successfully promote his own style of business and introduce it to more elegant places such as Knightsbridge and Mayfair.

But few customers came and he had to sack the manageress and take over her duties himself. Slowly, the venture continued to go pale and lifeless. It began to turn up at the corners and further cuts had to be made in the service that he offered. Then he was obliged to give the customers less value for their money – so they did not return. He had gambled everything on an enterprise that had failed to catch the imagination of those who could afford it. His reasoning in starting such a business in the first place had been unsound – nevertheless it had nudged him on. He had created a folly in his desire to "get rich quick". His dreams were of the possessions of the more wealthy and the comfortable ways of a life that was inherent therein. In the end all that remained were the undignified bruises on his self-esteem, and debts. An interesting footnote to that episode in his life is that many years later in 1974, McDonald's fast food restaurants opened their very first British branch not too many miles away, in Woolwich. As everyone knows, they now control a large empire throughout the United Kingdom – and one of that company's very successful shops is well placed in Kingston on Thames.

It was not to be long before Derek Tangye would turn his mind away from such aspirations and, together with his wife Jeannie, would seek a way of life that would parallel that of a poor tenant farmer who, each year, would harvest a main crop in the growth of personal contentment. But before then, Derek experienced a period of discontent that impressed his mood with a relentless negative bias – which, in turn, began to erode the relationship between him and Jeannie.

With the Savoy Hotel having re-established itself in a peacetime role, the clientèle had changed. No longer was there that friendly joking attitude that bounced around the corridors. Gone were the American journalists who awoke each war-ravaged day just glad to be alive – who looked forward to a coffee break with Jean Nicol in her office. The new breed of film stars and top entertainers from Broadway stood more at a distance – no longer one of the gang. The reasoning of departmental heads had also become different in their interpretations of running a peacetime hotel.

Jeannie found that her patience no longer stretched in as many different directions as it did in those days when survival depended on companionship at every level. She knew she was becoming disenchanted with her work in its post-war mode. Derek did not possess her strength and resilience, given their situation, and she found him hard to cope with at times. But a twinkling star had returned to shine in a darkening sky, which gave Jeannie someone to turn to – her sister Barbara had returned from Cairo in 1946.

The success of Derek Tangye's third book was worth little in terms of money, but it did bring in offers of work. The *Daily Express* gave him the opportunity to write the hugely popular William Hickey column. He was capable of such writing but he felt unsure of himself – it was the fact that he would have to "dig the dirt" once again that bothered him. The job required a mind that had no threshold to its conscience. It was also a prerequisite that the writer had a talent for reliable assumption and a nose that could smell ignominy on the wind. He accepted responsibility for the column and spent three days plumbing the principles of his virtuous upbringing – and then he quit. He decided he did not want to make a living off the backs of those he could expose for their incautious behaviour. Disclosures that were impacted with sufficient sensation for such a newspaper were few and not easy to come by. Marcel Proust had taught him that knowledge of such human emotions is shallow when it is begged from a faceless audience – to turn and face one's self would achieve a far greater sense of proportion. Derek had never been a hypocrite beyond what was normal to all mortals and he had never knowingly damaged the lives of others in a way that could be lasting.

In his next occupation he wrote the dialogue for a character called Judy in a strip cartoon for the *Daily Mail*, and in this he was extremely conscientious. But Judy was quite schizophrenic in that she took possession of his mind as he tried to create words that were handles to her thoughts. Wherever he was and whatever he did, he found himself constantly dwelling on her possible moods and the way she might express herself. So he banished Judy from his life and continued to write articles for any editor who would accept his work.

17

Derek and Jeannie Tangye realised their lives had changed to such a degree that they were unsure of continuing with enough control over what was left. Strangely, the spartan years of the war gave them direction in their demand for self-denial: when "too little" was savoured in a better sense of fulfilment than "too much". To say there was ambition would be wrong, especially in Derek's case, because he had never been truly enterprising by nature – with the exception of his pipe dream to attempt to build an empire of "take away" food shops, of course. They had entered the 1940s as a bachelor and a spinster – now, as the 1950s approached, they were bonded in just one identity. As such they were physically much stronger than in their former single status: with four hands, four arms, four legs and, most important, two heads that were blended in just one mind. They both agreed that the new post-war London had become harder to relate to. Derek, more so than Jeannie, needed something more positive to believe in as a way of life. If the Tangyes had been a farming family over the generations, he was now of the opinion that he would have settled quite comfortably into such a way of life. He felt, for the two of them, the tilling of the soil would give bumper crops of love and a happier peace of mind. They had health and strength and they believed in each other in a way that immortalised one in the other's mind. To remain in London, they imagined, would be to slowly die from the roots upward. If they were to plant those roots in mother nature's earth somewhere then, surely, there could be a new beginning.

After endless talking and discussions that often went late into the night, their enthusiasm became a horn of plenty that spilled over in the mind and they agreed that the life they both yearned for in their hearts was one and the same. Thames Bank Cottage at Mortlake took on the role of a GHQ as plans began to emerge. But first there had to be some reconnaissance if they were to relocate themselves. Holidays had been, thus far, always taken in Cornwall where they both knew a perfect kind of peace and tranquillity. And it being the county that held the seat of the Tangye generations, it was, for them, the perfect place in which to look.

In the spring of 1949 Jeannie decided she would resign her post as Publicity Manager with the Savoy Group of hotels, but she would wait until the end of the year before taking such action. In May they took a week's holiday and motored down to Lamorna cove in south-west Cornwall. The countryside was a carpet of new life and from the tiny harbour their minds were primed to quickly take note of things like the reflection of the sun as it shone on a sea of tiny turquoise waves. A small rivulet tumbled its way down a rough course of small granite boulders and flowed gently into the sea. On either side of the cove the rugged coastline rose high above the hamlet. A coastal path brought walkers into Lamorna from one direction and took them out on another – depending, of course, on which bearing they had made their approach in the first place.

On the first day of their holiday they enjoyed a quiet drink while sitting in front of Lamorna Inn. Local people smiled at them. They were all friendly and they had time for pleasant conversation – a gesture the Tangyes rarely encountered in London any more. The big city – where time always seemed to be in short supply, as though it were rationed, seemingly in fear that over demand would cause an even greater shortage; where the pace of life devalued time in human terms like yesterday's worthless currency and where the distance between the two points that represented the present moment and that of death was slowly contracting like an overstretched piece of elastic.

Derek and Jeannie Tangye were soon to realise that it could only be the Cornish way of life that would satisfy

120

them in their quest for self-sufficiency and give them absolute independence. The cliff path that would lead them towards the sun, they were told, would take them in the direction of Land's End:

an' long afore then there's some 'ansome ol' tumble' down cottage made from the granite on the cliff – but it ain't no good as it is! Got a little bit o' land with it mind you – but you'd have to be crazy or from up country to take on somethin' the likes of that. You both from Lon'on then?

Again, the author refers to the interview with Derek Tangye, in the living room of Dorminack (that was once that "ansome ol' tumble' down cottage"), in May 1992. Derek was asked, 'When you and Jeannie were staying at Lamorna Cove and you took that historic walk along the cliff path, you must have been surprised when you finally discovered the cottage – remote and abandoned – because it seems you didn't know it was there.'
Derek Tangye replied both promptly and keenly:

Oh yes we did. And when I was on that programme – the *Songs of Praise* programme – I read from the book *A Gull on the Roof* the moment when we did see it. We were standing on Carne Barges, which is the lovely solo rock overlooking Mount's Bay. We suddenly saw it and Jeannie said, 'There it is,' and then we saw in our minds all our figures criss-crossing in the years to come. It was a very magical moment.

Derek and Jeannie eventually secured the tenancy of the cottage for £25 per annum, which, in the beginning, included just a few acres of boulder-strewn land that mother nature had taken possession of and now looked reluctant to give up.
It is hard to imagine today, just how they could have inspected a cottage that was topped with a roof with more

121

holes in it than the pitted surface of the access lane and an interior that was wet enough to bring them down with chronic pneumonia – and still be fired with the same enthusiasm. They had both seen buildings disfigured in the London blitz and magically restored, fit enough for human habitation – and they knew in their hearts that Dorminack could rise again.

Before occupying the cottage there was a lot of spade work to be done – but first it had to have a new roof and they had no money. Water for drinking and cooking was to be taken from the stream that would become known as Monty's Leap. Washing water could be collected from rain draining off the roof – a new roof. A portable lavatory would serve for sanitation. Lighting would be by oil lamps and candles, and cooking would be on paraffin burners, one of which would also heat an oven made of tin plate. The only appliance that was modern for the day was a cumbersome wireless that was energised by a wet cell battery.

It seems beyond comprehension that two people, although disenchanted with their lives in a city mode, could of their own free will leave the comforts of a society that also offered a fair measure of security. They gave themselves in sacrifice to the gods of uncertainty, in a wilderness where they could be lost and forgotten and eventually even perish within the memory of their city friends. If Derek and Jeannie had been sentenced to serve a prison sentence breaking rocks, in hard labour, they would have at least been sure of bread and water. In Minack the land had first to be cleared of rocks to symbolically sow the seed for bread and if the stream dried up there would be no water. Such was their dedication and commitment to each other that they shared in a determination now to turn their backs on a style of life that others felt had served them well. A life of sophistication and fashion is acceptable to those who want competition in order to bring them challenge, so they may win superiority over others. But such a life did not make an allowance for Derek and Jeannie's quest for individuality.

So, while relatives and city friends became alarmed at their decision to lose themselves in the uncertainty of Minack, it became their expression to take hold of their own lives. It was the only way they could be sure of being able to manoeuvre the helm of the good ship destiny for themselves. They knew of the possibilities of insolvency and all that entailed. They believed in themselves and that was their strength – but they were also somewhat blind to their chances of total failure. Of course, personality traits were involved, and in this Jeannie was abundantly in credit. Derek was, indeed, fortunate to have discovered a partner in his life who was so willing and able to morally support him that she became his strength. He was selfish in his love for her and often restricted her freedom. Nevertheless, she accepted his whims with much sufferance. She understood him more than anyone else (more even than his own mother) and she devoted herself to him and their life at Minack.

Harold Thomas played an establishing role in Derek and Jeannie Tangye's life as flower and potato growers on the clifftop near Lamorna. He first met them after they had been told they could rent the cottage at Minack, together with its few acres of land, and they sought the services of a builder to reconstruct the roof, prior to their moving in.

Harold was a young man who was employed by his father, Ashley Thomas, in a family carpentry business that was based in their home village of St Buryan. And he remembers seeing Derek's tall and lean outline as it entered the yard accompanied by an extremely attractive and slim-figured young woman. Derek politely introduced himself and his wife, and informed Harold's father they had just taken on a property in the area, known as Dorminack. With luck, they had in Ashley Thomas an artist of his craft and an individual who was faithful to his given word. A man with a sympathetic ear, but a man who expected others to bide by the rules of *his* making – which meant, if he chose

123

to invoice his customers as many as 12 months *after* the completion of a job, then so be it. If the customer wished to clear his debt before Ashley had sent the long-awaited invoice, then it angered him.

On one such occasion, when the family sat at the meal table, Harold told his father of a customer who had been asking for a bill for the fitting of a new kitchen, as the man wished to keep his own accounting in order. Ashley Thomas immediately got to his feet, his jowls set solid in annoyance. He placed his knife and fork heavily and noisily onto his plate – he had no appetite now and his meal was ruined.

'That's all some people can think about,' he complained, like a man who had just suffered a gross miscarriage of justice. 'Bloody money!' And then he walked briskly from the room.

Derek explained to the Thomases the task that awaited at Dorminack – the most urgent of jobs being the roof. Tentative plans were drawn up and the need for materials discussed. It was arranged that Harold, together with his father, would start immediately by making a site visit. As the couple left the yard, Jeannie was heard to say, 'Didn't you ought to tell Mr Thomas?'

'Tell me what?' the master carpenter enquired.

Derek Tangye looked somewhat abashed – almost guilty. 'We haven't got any money,' he confessed.

'Oh – can you manage to pay by instalments?' came a proposition.

If Derek had been honest, he was unsure of *any* of his financial matters at that moment in time, but he *was* desperate to have a new roof on the cottage – one that could stand the ravages of the worst of the Cornish winter gales. He acknowledged his benefactor in his gratitude.

'That would be very generous and I'm most grateful to you.'

Within four weeks Dorminack had a topping-out ceremony to celebrate a new roof that was economically constructed of corrugated asbestos. A roof, in its basic composition, that was symbolic of the austere life in which Derek and Jeannie would now dwell.

The task of land husbandry that lay ahead of them was gargantuan. Many acres of overgrown meadow had to be rapidly cleared and planted – almost by hand. And they discovered that it was not only in the big city that time could sometimes be *more* than money – in their initial struggle to establish themselves at Minack and to quickly get some kind of a return from the land, time had become a formidable opponent in rural Cornwall also.

A Cornishman's generosity can indeed become a newcomer's bounty and the Tangyes discovered just that in Tommy Williams, who was a "rustic" living in a caravan in a field near St Buryan. He was learned in his understanding of the countryside and the creatures it contained. Even before Derek and Jeannie had finally abandoned London, he had worked for them three days a week – singlehanded and throughout a cold clifftop winter. He cleared the meadows and tamed the wild and overgrown hedges. He built windbreak fencing from the cuttings of the trees he had cropped back and improved the access track that led from the lane to the cottage – there he even planted colourful flowers as a welcome for when they finally settled in.

There were to be a few other gemstones in local Cornish people who would, at some time, work for Derek and Jeannie Tangye on a part or full-time basis. They were admirable souls whose support would contribute greatly to the control of Minack as a new frontier. Yet the time would come when Derek's unreasonable and, fortunately, just occasional outbursts of his former arrogance in a difference of an opinion, would be responsible for the rapid dissolving of a treasured friendship. And if he were to approach an individual once more, after such a breach, it would only be if he was in need of his or her special skills – after he had been unsuccessful in replacing that person with another. There were occasions when Jeannie became an anchor and she was able to prevent a rift from occurring. Of those

125

occasions, Derek sometimes reproached himself when writing the *Minack Chronicles* – if he felt the incident was worth a mention, that is. With an inverted awareness of himself he would attempt to justify his own circumstance through the convenience of his typewriter.

A thousand revellers celebrated at a New Year's Eve ball in the Savoy Hotel when, on Big Ben's twelfth chime of midnight, they optimistically and noisily welcomed in the unblemished year of 1950: a year when Princess Anne would be born in Clarence House, in London. Now it was the start of a new decade and for the Tangyes it was to be a fresh beginning. Derek quietly anticipated the coming 12 months and he felt the hand of destiny pulling him forward. He had no spiritual vision, just a compelling intuition that now the time was right for them to cross that line of clear distinction between their past and their future.

Now, with a new roof firmly in place on the cottage, a good supply of water in the stream, and an Elsan chemical toilet installed in an outhouse, they would be able to dedicate themselves to a completely new way of life at Minack.

As the New Year's revelry continued, Jeannie lifted a bottle of champagne from the ice bucket on her table and took it, together with some novelties and paper hats, to the young ladies who staffed the cloakroom. She took a first footing over the threshold of room 205 and, with a glistening of a tear in each eye for times remembered, she gently closed the door and Derek gladly took her to Thames Bank Cottage at Mortlake – a place that had, by now, become a mere staging post on their journey to Cornwall.

The door she had closed was not just on a room that contained the past ten years of her working life, but it was also, symbolically, on those dear souls who had walked into her life there and warmed her heart with their precious friendship and love. The parties and the over-indulgences would now remain as ghostly images, accommodated within those four walls. As a young woman conscious of her health and her slim figure, she would no longer have to eat or drink too much to be hospitable in the call of her duty.

The following morning she was back in room 205, where she typed her resignation and took it to Mr Thornewill. He sat in silence for a few moments as he read the letter. He placed it on his desk and looked at her in the manner of her father.

'You are a very exceptional young woman with a wonderful career ahead of you – is this *really* what you want to do?'

Jeannie nodded silently – she felt more determined than at any other time in her life. Mr Thornewill smiled kindly at her.

'Of course, I shall ask you to think again – if you will not, then, along with all at the Savoy Hotel, I shall wish you luck and every happiness – we will *all* miss you.'

As Jeannie opened the door of his office to leave, he softly cleared his throat as if asking for her attention once again.

'Oh – and please give Captain Tangye my kind regards – he's a *very* lucky man – indeed.'

18

Derek and Jeannie Tangye looked curiously like nomad tinkers as their canvas-topped Land Rover trundled down the uneven track at Minack – like a covered wagon of early frontier settlers. The canvas bulged with pots and pans, suitcases, blankets, and an ironing board – even an armchair. It was midnight on Good Friday, 7 April 1950. When they arrived, darkness had long since covered the clifftop meadows and a full moon was casting night-time shadows there. Before them was a fantasia that was fired of their own imaginations. Everything they could see was clean, crisp and mint fresh, with a lustre that would disappear as the moon would gradually ebb in the night sky. Carne Barges sat in solid granite, like a revered image of worship that had been eroded and shaped by the atmospheric elements of a million years or more – it was burnished like old copper in the light of the moon. Far in the distance the silhouette of St Michael's Mount rose magically out of a glinting sea like a wizard's castle. In the morning light all that would look different yet again and the meadows would reveal a wild and alluring picture that would impassion them every bit as much. In their togetherness, they felt romantic in a way that exceeded the bounds of all tender love. Somewhere, in a field close by, Cornish piskeys danced in a circle of upright granite rocks that were the myth of the Merry Maidens. As Derek and Jeannie crossed the threshold of the cottage at Minack they both knew that Cornwall was, for them, the promised land – and, at long last, they had completed their sentimental journey home.

All the way from London Monty had sat calmly on Jeannie's lap, cushioned from the bumps of the Land Rover. He was their marmalade striped cat and their vibes told him all was well. He would become celebrated on the book-shelves of homes the world over and he would share in some of their success at Minack. But, before then, he would witness their desperation also. In the strongest will to succeed, it seems, there is a need to be fired up through the experience of wretched suffering – and there would be such times, as they would endeavour to live off the land and on a budget of just two pounds and ten shillings per week.

The following morning all the glory of Minack reached in to them as the sun shone through the uncurtained bedroom window. They had spent a night of velvet sleep on a mattress on the floor – Monty was curled up at their feet. Behind their euphoria was a feeling that told them they had spent years as hostages in a modern society that had now released them.

That first Easter Saturday morning they began a life on what seemed to them to be another planet that was well placed in a brilliant assembly of new stars. They would till the land and encourage its growth and protect all life that was God-given. Jeannie would seek to ensure that not one creature would die there by the hand of a human being. There would be just one law and one only within their dominion – that in the name of freedom. Freedom of thought, freedom of expression and freedom to breathe the air that nourished all within Minack. For Derek the past was now an old and shabby coat that he no longer needed. And in that very image, 1950 was, coincidentally, the year of the centenary celebrations of the bowler hat – the very hat which, for him, was one of the symbols of false expression he had gladly left behind in London.

It was appropriate that, shortly after their arrival at Minack, at the end of May, on a warm and still evening they listened to the serialised radio programme "The Arch-ers" on the BBC airwaves. Throughout the country, from that very first episode, listeners identified with the charac-ters and their utterances as they applauded the simple and contented village life of their own unspoken longing. As Derek and Jeannie sat in the garden listening to the wireless through an opened window they too, in their hearts, lived with the characters who coped, through the studio microphone, with their problems and celebrated their joys – in a way that was, one day, to become the *Minack Chronicles*.

As a former journalist Derek had difficulty in suppressing his curiosity for news of events at home and abroad. He had chosen *not* to live in the everyday world of the lemming, but he still had a need of mind for what went on in it. It was commonplace that such reporting was on the dramas of life. The human mind possesses an inherent inquisitiveness that is gratified only by the production of such a negative bias. Crying, it suggests, is more potent to the emotions than laughter. But this is where the *Minack Chronicles*, just like the early editions of "The Archers", were to pioneer another standard – they recycled self-pity and hopelessness and showed there could be a law of alternatives. In this philosophy, at Minack, Jeannie became the producer and Derek was both the playwright and the director.

Dreams fall into two different categories: those of anxiety and desire – and it is from this basic foundation that the symbolism of sleepers' fantasies are analysed and interpreted, not the fairy-tale fiction that so often appears in less informed publications. If we had total control over the events in our lives we would not choose those which would cause us terrible anxieties. Instead, we would look for those which would bring us the happiness and the satisfaction of our desires. To favour violence would indicate a flaw in the mind and a quirk of the personality. It is anticipated, therefore, that to be a dependable reader of the *Minack Chronicles* is, likely, never to be one of life's pathetic aggressors – for the Minack followers are surely guided by their love and compassion for other beings.

As Derek and Jeannie Tangye continued to settle into their peaceful lives in Cornwall, war broke out in Korea. With an invading North Korean army supported by Chinese communist troops trying to overrun the independent and democratic southern half of the country, the battle was taken up by the United Nations Organisation who quickly mobilised a composite fighting force of many nations, of which the United States of America and the United Kingdom became the main defenders of freedom and democracy. There was a General Election, and the results were televised for the very first time: a Labour Government was returned, but with a much reduced majority.

Derek Tangye, by influence of heritage, had been essentially right-wing in his views but he was inclined to give the impression in the *Minack Chronicles* that he sat legs astride a political fence, symbolically with his left foot touching down on one side and his right foot on the other. He was a traditionalist who championed the cause of law and order, but he often possessed a silent sympathy for the underdog. He had strict views on common (not moralising) decency. He was intolerant of conversationalists with views and attitudes that were in conflict with his own and, as a result, he became a patient listener to orators who reflected similar opinions to his own. He was a genial host to those who did not overstay their welcome when visiting Minack. But he was not the diplomat that his wife had learned to be in her days as the head of public relations at the Savoy Hotel. In fact, the practice of selection through discretion never seemed an integral part of his thinking which, when you think about it, made him an unusual candidate for circumspect involvement with the security services of MI5.

Today, as a cottage, Dorminack is celebrated and, to those who have searched it out, it presents itself as a theatrical high point in the image of the *Minack Chronicles* and it has made a valued contribution to modern Cornish history. It was inhabited by a succession of families in the nineteenth century and it would appear that each one had remained there in residence for about ten years – but there *were* exceptions. In its original capacity as a working man's home, it depended on the cast-iron Cornish cooking range that was still tucked away in the living room when the Tangyes moved in. It once had two storeys and it also had a thatched roof. It caught fire and burned down in 1912 – the year Derek was born. Evidence suggests that, in each generation of dwellers, the wage earner worked as an agricultural labourer or as a dairyman. However, research on the part of this author has added to the chronicles of that history. In the late nineteenth century Harry Ladner married Mary Trewern and he carried her over the Dorminack threshold. The cottage must have had two storeys because the couple had four children, each of whom was born and married there. This author talked to one of the grandchildren, who still lives in south-west Cornwall. His mother was born there in 1906 as Elsie Ladner – she had two sisters, Doris and Gladys, and one brother Henry (Henry was to become a local farmer). Harry Ladner died at Dorminack and Mary passed away there less than a decade later.

The cottage soon became the home of a countrywoman named Kathleen Badger. Local knowledge tells that she was still there in 1947, having previously provided a safe wartime haven for a mother and her two young sons who were evacuated there from London. After that, the cottage stood empty for a while, when it deteriorated badly and became unfit for human habitation.

It seems that Derek and Jeannie Tangye were the first couple not to have children with them in the cottage. This had been a conscious decision on their part. But in the lonely years after Jeannie's death, Derek did express his regret at not having the comfort of a grown-up family of his own – someone tied by blood and to whom he could leave his goods and chattels. It seemed to him so impersonal, under an auctioneer's hammer, to dispose of a lifetime's meaningful existence. And when such an event did take place, Minack's trustees became faithfully obliged to become bidders in order to save certain items in the memory of both Derek and Jeannie Tangye.

Through the mesmerising pages of the *Minack Chronicles*, readers were inspired to face themselves and to climb

132

over obstacles instead of turning back. Some learned how
to accept a disabling illness and to cope with the mental
strains of each day. Derek was their strength – or so they
believed. In reality, that strength was Jeannie's. He wrote
words to music she had already scored through her strength
and inspiration. Without her, he would have trundled
through his life continuously searching and never being
quite sure of what he was looking for. She did not try to
dominate him or control his mind. She did not try to
manipulate him – his mind was free. She stimulated him
and he became a carriage of her energy: this he translated
into the words that aroused his readers. Together they
expressed the conviction of his writing – but the seat of the
courage was indeed hers.

Derek lived with a shrouded sense of insecurity: like a
boatman with a pint-sized bailer trying to cope with a two-
pint leak. Those around saw him as an old romantic who
was often over-possessive with his wife. Each Thursday
morning, immediately after breakfast, Jeannie left Dorminack and drove along the track that led her to the main
road, where she turned to the right and travelled on towards
the hamlet of Sheffield, near Newlyn. Once there, she
parked the car outside a telephone box and rang her sister
Barbara in Derbyshire. In the early Minack days, when
there was little money for extras, Barbara paid for the call
by having the charges reversed. Afterwards, Jean drove on
into Penzance and parked in the public car park beside the
municipal offices at St John's Hall, and from there she took
a few minute's walk to George Trewhella's butcher's shop
– a visit she always looked forward to because there she
spent ten minutes ordering meat and exchanging friendly
banter. This shopping expedition was a routine that was
performed each week and, as she was always too early for
the bank, George Trewhella provided her with the service
of giving her cash back on her cheque. She always looked
forward to those visits with George's good-hearted teasing.
While he got her order together she kept a regular appointment with the hairdresser. It was always the same routine,

and when she arrived home to Dorminack Derek was always waiting impatiently for her. Later he bought her a home hairdryer and the time of her Thursday visit to Penzance was reduced accordingly.

Derek Tangye remained cool in his attitude towards Jeannie's parents for the continuation of their lives – for he was aware that he had ceased to be an option in their approval as a son-in-law from the moment they had read his book *Time Was Mine*. Also, he foolishly allowed his feelings for Jeannie's sister Barbara and her husband Richard to be tainted. On the occasions of a marriage in Barbara's family, Jeannie always travelled to Derbyshire alone – and Derek remained doggedly entrenched at Minack. On one such visit she stayed over an extra night, having let him know of her intention. On her return to Penzance railway station there was to be no warm greeting. Instead, she was confronted by a disconsolate spouse – contrary in his apparent affection for her and unwilling to communicate in reasonable conversation. Jeannie had other such difficult moments with Derek in the course of their life together. She had discovered very early in their marriage that he could abandon himself, in just that way, to negative emotion. At such times she did not allow herself the indignity of an humiliating confrontation. She told her sister, after one such occasion, that her love for him was strong enough to absorb the impact of his moods and she would never be influenced to consider leaving him – no matter what.

Derek Tangye was indeed a very fortunate man to have a wife who was unseeded with the same fraught emotions that took possession of him from time to time. In such moments Jeannie turned to Carne Barges. This composition of an upward rising granite rock sparked a metamorphosis in her perception. She prayed there. She had spiritual communication there. She cleansed her mind there and, in the rock pool at the bottom of the cliff, she sometimes bathed naked and cleansed her body there.

As an individualist, Derek was sometimes unwittingly like

134

a member of a society that was so secret that it held no meetings and had no gathering place. As such, he sought no corporate body to represent him either, for that would encourage a blanket of dependency that would, in turn, stifle him. People who thrive within a team spirit may find those words difficult to understand – but such, also, is the plight of the individualist in the teamster's world.

Most of those who were attracted to become involved with Minack over the Tangye perennial years were, in fact, themselves individualists – although they may not have been fully aware of such a potential at that time. Two fine examples were Jane and Shelagh. The two girls were still in the years that had not yet reached full maturity, and they carried their distinction as individualists well. Both preferred the company of animals to that of prime beings. Shelagh lived in a caravan with her dogs near St Buryan. Jane lived with her mother and brother and a variety of animals, just a short distance from Dorminack in an old farm worker's cottage that was perched high on the cliff. In the summer the sun shone warmly down and new life was created all around. In winter the strong winds lifted off the sea to the clifftop meadows where nature had already become a sleeping repository.

To be normal was to accept the conventions of what was seen to be an urbane society – and in her young years Jane was not prepared to do that blindly. Some saw her as being something of a maverick who revealed herself by constantly standing back from the potential of a token flag of truce – that, to her, would have conditions she did not wish to comply with. Such was an important part of her growing up and such was her choice. Today, with a capacity for intelligent introspection, she looks back on those early years with a different comprehension from her adolescent attitude – and also with a philosophy that is now well reasoned. But on the other side of the coin, she realises there were missed opportunities, where she denied herself conversations with many famous and interesting people who came to stay as guests of Minack.

Jeannie understood Jane and the two worked well together, whether in the meadows or in the packing shed. Conversations were happy and light-hearted and Jeannie was known for her giggling. It was in those early days when hard work was plentiful, and when there was little in return, that the true spirit of Minack was born.

When Jane worked in the clifftop meadows it was always without a watch on her wrist and she judged the time according to the punctual passing of the passenger-carrying boat, the *Scillonian*. The vessel left Penzance harbour at the same time each morning and made its way to the Scilly Isles, returning later in the day. When the sun shone Jane pushed a stick into the soil to cast a shadow as a basic form of sundial. Author and philosopher A.P. Herbert was a friend and popular visitor to Minack, where he often stayed. He would roll up his shirtsleeves and help in the meadows. He and Jane worked well together and the generation gap was bridged with the conversation of similar minds. He was intrigued by her method of timekeeping and she fondly remembers how he pushed a second stick into the soil and showed her how to keep time even more accurately.

Jane realised the value of a good education but, for her, it was a passport that was not needed to progress in the sort of life she anticipated for herself. Her job at Minack had saved her from being packed off to boarding school and, like Derek, she possessed no desire to achieve supremacy over others through academic challenge and competition. But true individualism is not about dropping out – it takes strength and courage to swim against the flow that engulfs all who are the willing participants in a society with a herd instinct.

'We had destiny,' Derek Tangye exclaimed to each and every one as they read the *Minack Chronicles*. Such was the statement he also made to those of his readers who visited him at the cottage. He spoke in a past tense that told how, as a result of Minack, destiny had now been achieved. A lifetime's wanderlust and searching had ended the day he and Jeannie had gingerly pushed open the creaking door of a tumbled down Dorminack – and furtively peered inside. All the frustrations of a lifetime that had been uncertain, and all the anxieties that had stifled a mind that was seeking to be inspired, disappeared in that second it took to cross the threshold. Derek knew he had lived his life for Jeannie and that moment they walked together through the door-way. They had brought their memories with them as part of their possessions – it was their stock in hand ready for when they would both write. Memories are often some of life's most precious possessions, but they are worthless as collateral to a bank manager – until you use them to write a best-selling book, of course.

Derek and Jeannie rebuilt Dorminack and they reconstructed their lives at the same time. Their immortality is spiritual and it will continue to exist for as long as that granite cottage will lay either on or under the soil of Minack – and those who seek Oliver Land will continue to arrive on a curious and tranquil path of discovery.

But God, in his wisdom, placed frailties in the minds of all mortals without exception. Jeannie was unsympathetic towards illness. Her conviction was one of mind over matter and in this she had a list of scores to her credit. However, her own achievements caused her sometimes to forget the limitations of the human body. Barbara took the occasional holiday in Lamorna Cove after her first husband had died, and the two sisters were able to spend valued time together. But as they walked the cliff path on one occasion Barbara fell heavily. She instinctively put her hands forward to cushion her fall and she broke one of her wrists in three places. Feeling the pain and sensing the nature of the injuries, she asked Jeannie to drive her to the Casualty Department at the hospital in Penzance. But Jeannie was unsympathetic and refused – she suggested the wrist was merely sprained. On the following day X-rays revealed the fractures.

Barbara had known true love with her first husband and her bereavement undermined her emotionally. She assumed that, having known the feeling of such devotion once, another love could not tread the same path – and in this she was wrong. She had known Richard Bamford as a dear friend for many years and, as she mourned her husband, he was at her side to comfort her. In time they became close. Much later, romance came to them and he proposed to her. In her heart she knew she had been blessed once again. But she needed to let go of her first husband's love, enough to show Richard that she could love him too. Jeannie already knew Richard and she saw that her sister was on the brink of happiness once more. In the soft light of the evening she walked to Carne Barges and she prayed for Barbara – who returned to Derbyshire and to wedding bells.

19

In the mind's eye, undertakers are seen to be sombre men in dark suits, who contrive to express a deep sympathy for the bereaved. Often, they talk in gentle voices that are lowered in tone and display manners that are more polite than those of a kindly church warden. Harold Thomas had none of these traits, bar the politeness – but he *was* an undertaker. He could tell a funny story and laugh heartily as part of its deliverance. He had a piskey sense of all things mischievous and he was good company. His tongue was curled in the true sound of a Cornishman. As carpenters, he and his father made coffins – so it followed that, in a small country community like St Buryan, he should be an undertaker also.

In the early Tangye settlement days, when Harold and his father capped Dorminack with a new roof, they later converted an old chicken house which was attached to the side of the cottage. The extension became a second bedroom, with an adjoining bathroom and lavatory. Such a task meant drilling through a 60-centimetre granite wall to create an adjoining doorway with the cottage. And the improvements brought Dorminack more in line with twentieth-century needs for human habitation.

Harold was often retained at Minack as a jobbing carpenter. But this was usually at a time when his own business was quiet. Through his skills he transformed much of the cottage and the surrounding outbuildings. After each job had been completed, Derek would express his appreciation by remarking, 'Harold – you're a bloody wonderman.' But Derek's mood could change and it sometimes created a feeling of tension which would stretch a friendship thin. And like some of the others who came to know him, Harold

139

also was eventually to form an opinion that 'He was a funny old bugger!'

Another part-timer in those early days at Minack was later to become the coxswain of the Sennen lifeboat. He could turn his hand to many things and worked as a carpenter's mate to Harold Thomas when he was asked by Derek to build a cupboard in the small master bedroom of the cottage. Each working day in Cornwall, in the morning, somewhere between the hours of ten and eleven o'clock, work comes to a temporary halt for a tea break that is known as "Croust time". This coincided with some business the Tangyes had to attend to in Penzance on the day of the cupboard making. But, before they left, Jeannie, attentive as always, apologised to the two men that she did not have the time to make them tea. There was, instead, home-made cider stored in the cool of one of the stone outbuildings – and, if they wished, they could help themselves.

"Croust time" on that day became very special indeed, as the two men inadvertently drank from the wrong flagon. They had chosen one that contained a more potent cider, and as they sat in conversation they were tempted to have another glass – and another – and yet another.

'This is mighty good stuff,' remarked the coxswain.

When the time came to resume work Harold stood up and promptly fell to the ground – his legs would not support him. The other man tried – he could only get as far as his knees and eventually gave up. Had the Tangyes returned at that moment, Jeannie would have laughed at the scene of a silent movie comedy – but both men knew Derek would have expressed his annoyance at their silliness. They sat on the ground like two Guy Fawkes dummies, backs against the wall with two pairs of useless legs stretching forward – and there they had no alternative but to wait patiently. Eventually, they were able to haul themselves to a standing position. But, by then, time had run very short and the cupboard had to be completed in a hurry. Almost as the last screw was being driven into the last hinge, Derek's

140

voice was heard to boom from the bedroom doorway. 'Harold – you're a bloody wonderman!'

'Did you like the cider?' Jeannie asked the two men.

'It was some 'andsome stuff,' said Harold.

Derek stepped forward and tried opening one of the cupboard doors. 'I say – this is a bit tight.'

Harold noticed there was a glint in Jeannie's eye as she excused the incompletion of the job on his part. 'I'm sure that will be seen to tomorrow when Harold comes back to paint it.'

When Derek had driven the car into the parking space between two of the outbuildings on their return, Jeannie had noticed an empty cider flagon discarded on the ground, where the two men had previously been stranded with lifeless limbs.

Derek's first writing studio at Minack was a modest wooden shed that measured seven feet by five feet. It had been erected on a ledge where the meadow cliffs lowered to the sea, giving a magnificent panoramic view of Mount's Bay. The first time he went inside, he looked through the picture window and saw the white sails of little boats on blue water – each vessel was finding the going difficult as it tried to race in the gentle breeze of the waters that surrounded St Michael's Mount. He looked across the bay to the south-east, to Lizard Point – from where, in 1901, the very first wireless transmissions were made across the Atlantic Ocean to Guglielmo Marconi, as he waited, keen to receive them, in Newfoundland.

Derek savoured the peace of mind he had discovered there and the little hut filled him with inspiration. In a few days he would begin to write the first of the *Minack Chronicles*: *A Gull on the Roof*. But before then he would get Harold Thomas to paint the floor of the shed with a pesticide to stop the ants that were finding their way up through the tiny gaps in the boards. The sun had already climbed high enough in the sky to observe Harold as he arrived the following morning to begin the job. A pot containing creosote and a new brush had been thoughtfully placed beside the door of the shed for him. The sea had changed its colour a little and was now a pleasant turquoise, the sky was blue, and the inside temperature of the wooden hut continued to rise as the sun climbed yet higher – the fumes became stifling. Harold's head ached a little but he pressed on because he was keen to finish the job – then he could breathe as much of the good fresh air that came off the bay as he wanted.

The job done, he sat in the open, relieved to be purging his lungs once more. Derek and Jeannie passed him by as he sat on a rock beside the path. They had come to admire his work. Then there came a roar like that of an angered lion that had run amok inside the shed. The creosote and the midday heat had caused the interior to become a gas chamber and it was estimated it would take months before it would become clear once again. No one knows who placed the creosote beside the door, implying that it was the required ant deterrent. The pesticide was later found inside a lean-to that was attached to the outbuilding where the cider was kept. Over the coming weeks the creosote fumes were closely monitored and plans to begin writing in the hut were abandoned. The book was eventually started in a small building that was hurriedly cleared to become yet another studio and was later to be known as the Confusion Room. From there the panoramic view was of the clifftop meadows, which compensated for the partial loss of the sea view. And what was the fate of that wooden writing room on the clifftop ledge? It became overgrown with blackthorn and brambles and was, in time, consumed entirely by mother nature in the teeth of harsh winter gales.

It was never easy for Derek Tangye to conceal his anger or the petty intolerances that he sometimes felt. And it was unfortunate that he allowed such feelings to erode good relationships and to lose him valued friendships. With no thought of the benevolence shown by Harold Thomas and his father in the help they had given him to become established in Cornwall, he was to terminate Harold's occupational association there and to ask him to leave Minack.

There had been several incidents but the barb that was finally to tear the flesh of kind regard between the two men was that of Derek's anger. It erupted in a disagreement over a large glazed porch that Harold Thomas had been asked to build on the side of the cottage a few years previously, one that generously covered the area of the main door. When Harold began hammering out the holes in the stone wall, he had advised Derek that climatic conditions at Minack were such that, although the wood had been treated, there would always be a risk of the frame rotting with time, just where it was inserted into the wall – and there would be a need for a regular inspection. He was to remark about this need on numerous occasions, suggesting that he should take a look, but Derek constantly postponed the investigation and, when rot did appear, he chose to seek the services of another tradesman whose own remedial treatment did not work. In an outburst of anger he blamed Harold for the rot starting in the first place and he dispensed with his services in a moment's notice – and severed a valued friendship. The porch was replaced with a glazed conservatory that served as a dining-room and also as an outer chamber in which to receive visitors to Dormi-nack. Derek had, once again, discovered a tradesman who, like all others at their very best, possessed a craftman's skill that was good but could only equal that of Harold Thomas.

There are countless readers of the chronicles, the world over, who feel privileged to share the vision of Minack. It was an embodiment of a Shangri-la that was achieved through the challenge it presented, in the first place, to Derek and Jeannie. Those readers possess a very personal feeling of realistically sharing in the life there. They are all special members of a Tangye fellowship and he continues to release them from the drudgery of their everyday lives as they become absorbed in any one of his books. It is possible some of those people may be dismayed to learn that he could behave with such a negative attitude towards others.

143

But if they perceive his writing more profoundly they will interpret a few of those moments when he dares to seek them as his confessor. He subconsciously encourages those readers to discover the impetus that has motivated him throughout his life – something he understood so little in himself.

Jeannie wanted to have some extra shelves built into her kitchen, which was the size of a small ship's galley. Harold Thomas was making a few notes as he measured up for the task when Derek entered the room and enquired what he was doing there. Jeannie intervened with an explanation. Derek's words to her were harsh as he told her there was no room for more shelves – and Harold was gruffly dismissed from the cottage. Jeannie possessed such strength that she did not react in her own anger, but she was, nevertheless, highly embarrassed.

Before his dismissal, Harold Thomas arrived for work each morning astride his old Sunbeam motorcycle; and often riding the pillion was his good mate, the lifeboat coxswain. Minack sometimes presented a Christmas card picture of pristine white in the winter as a hoar frost laid a sparkling carpet over the meadows and veiled the drystone walls that bordered the lanes. On one occasion, as the two men dismounted and parked the motorcycle beside an outhouse where the seedling potatoes were stacked in trays ready to shoot, they both noticed the door had been left open. Derek, who always noticed their arrival, came to talk to them. When he saw the door was open he accused them of leaving it that way the day before. Jeannie was already in the packing shed and when she heard the commotion she joined them, confessing that it was she who had absent-mindedly left it like that overnight. Derek's response was pitiful in his over-reaction. He shouted aloud, 'Jeannie, what have you done? We're ruined – we're ruined!'

They were, at that particular time, having great financial problems, which worried them both deeply, and the incident was to Jeannie's regret because she knew they could ill afford the risk of such a mistake. But it was also to her

144

credit that she did not feed his anger through her own response. Such was the measure of a truly remarkable lady, who was able to maintain that same dignity in every like encounter with her husband. As a footnote, an investigation showed, however, that the frost had not harmed the potato shoots in any way. On paper the Tangyes were, indeed, already ruined – and it would take the unfolding and the publishing of the *Minack Chronicles* to counter that situation, and to continue with a measure of prosperity.

20

Soon after arriving at Minack, Jeannie settled down to write her first book, *Meet Me At The Savoy*, which was autobiographical. It centred around her life as the head of public relations for the Savoy Hotel Group. It also featured the famous people she came to know and the historical wartime events that took place there. It is amazingly comprehensive in its detail of names and occurrences. Unbelievably, several large publishers turned the manuscript down and it was eventually taken up by the much smaller Museum Press, in 1952. That publisher was soon to discover that it had a bestseller on its list. But its success did not mean that it made an amazingly large amount of money for her, although the book sales *did* ease the financial problems somewhat.

Prior to that event, Derek's brother Nigel opened the magnificent family home of Glendorgal, that overlooked Porth Beach in Cornwall, as a summer hotel and restaurant, with a fine qualifying status. This was done under the ownership of their mother who, as a widow, shared in its income. She died in 1954 and Glendorgal was inherited, in equal shares, by her three sons.

In 1955, Derek began writing *A Gull On The Roof*. Once again, when it was finished it was difficult to find a publisher – until the house of Michael Joseph recognised its potential and the book found its way onto the shelves in 1961. It met with a success that established the beginning of the *Minack Chronicles*.

Back in that year of 1955, Nigel became the sole owner of Glendorgal, as a hotel, by buying his two brothers out. This happened at a time when Derek was receiving depressing letters from his bank manager, and his share of Glendorgal meant that he could enjoy a period of respite in his concern that his cheques might not be honoured. But the financial problems were only suppressed, because extreme competition and the overnight contradictions of market prices for produce such as flowers and potatoes made it hard to earn a living while, at the same time, retaining their dependant employees. Just as Derek was in his earlier life, so he was still inclined to be sluggish in settling his accounts with those who supplied Minack. It was an irresponsible way with him that had always frustrated his mother. Now it affected Jeannie, in the same way that constantly dripping water could wear away stone.

Good fortune, of the human kind, came to Minack in 1956. Geoffrey Semmens became a good and faithful worker, capable of managing every aspect of the Minack business. It meant that Derek and Jeannie now had the freedom to make the occasional journey to London, safe in the knowledge that their crops would not suffer. Geoffrey was a young man strong in limb and experienced in his craft. When he married Emily it brought new romance to Minack and the happiness, in anticipation of the wedding, reflected in Jeannie's mood as she made posies for the bridesmaids. For so many years the clifftop meadows had been wild, controlled by the will of nature. Now Minack lived again, with voices that laughed in the fields and packing shed. And, as in the days of the Ladner family, another wedding meant another celebration.

As Derek and Jeannie became celebrities they were invited throughout south-west Cornwall to official dinners. They opened fetes and presented prizes and silver cups at sporting functions. Wherever they went people smiled and wanted to say hallo – to ask how the cats or the donkeys in the meadow were. Children's voices rang out happily when they were invited to Minack to the celebration of the donkeys' birthday parties in Oliver Land. And television crews came from far horizons to film the spectacle of such events.

Derek was known to speak openly, on occasions, to employees about the income from sales. He also possessed

147

a sense of compassion that could reveal itself in a crisis. He knew, from personal experience, of the rancid smell of being penniless – a smell that got up the smug noses of many who were, themselves, comfortably off. And he scorned the ignorance of people who were inclined to look down on those who suffered the stigma of such poverty. When fate turns unkindly around and bites back at its beholder the result can be one of tragedy. Providence did just that when Geoffrey and Emily Semmens lost their home in a devastating fire – and all their possessions were destroyed. Derek immediately came to their aid with help that included making a solicitor available, should they need legal assistance – and it has to be said that his benevolence was at a time when he and Jeannie were still not totally financially secure themselves. Geoffrey had not been able to afford a car so the Land Rover was lent to him each weekend. And despite Derek's occasional outbursts of intolerance, Geoffrey found him an easygoing boss.

There was also an occasion when Emily had to attend the hospital in Redruth, more than 21 miles distant. Her mother-in-law accompanied her to care for her children and this made the taxi ride expensive. Derek covered the total cost of that journey.

But it seems that the flip side of the coin was always ready to show itself. In 1960, the year before Derek Tangye's book *A Gull On The Roof* was published – and a time when he needed his dependable employees even more – he claimed he could no longer afford to pay overtime or supply the staff with a drink of tea each day. As Geoffrey already gave more time than he was paid for, he challenged Derek in his unfairness and as a result he was told to leave. As Geoffrey gathered his belongings to leave, Derek watched, knowing he had probably condemned himself to the stern reality of his own folly.

Over the following four years Derek tried in vain to replace Geoffrey Semmens with someone as talented and hard-working, but no such a person was available. So, in 1964, he humbly sat down and, without apologising for his previous hasty action in dismissing him, he wrote Geoffrey a letter asking that he return to work at Minack. Geoffrey accepted and was reinstated, to continue his work as though he had never left off.

Jeannie disliked housework; she was far happier toiling in the meadows or busily packing the produce in the sheds. So, also in 1964, Emily became employed to clean the cottage for her on a part-time basis. As with all employees, Derek insisted that he and Jeannie were to be known as Mr and Mrs Tangye – a quirk that had followed him from his days using the Savoy Hotel when, to Jeannie's horror, he coldly called the staff by their own surnames with the pomposity of a military zealot.

Each working day, Jeannie thoughtfully collected Emily from her home and returned her there when she had finished her work. Once more the Semmens became Minack minders when their employers took a nostalgic return trip to the Savoy Hotel in London. There were animals, both domesticated and wild, to care for and crops to tend. There was also the postman to look out for. One letter was delivered which had OHMS printed on the envelope and it was from the taxman. Years later when Emily recalled the event, it seemed to her that she had been naive in her behaviour. Because she thought the letter had looked important, she forwarded it to the Savoy Hotel. It was also much later before Derek was able to feel amused by that same occasion – which almost ruined their trip down memory lane in the capital, a time when they had wished to leave all worrying money matters behind and out of mind.

Eventually, Emily was to have a change of boss in a sideways move. She gave up cleaning the cottage of Dorminack for Jeannie and took on a job in the packing shed, and there she came under Derek's jurisdiction. All who were involved with packing enjoyed the happy times of light-hearted conversation. They discussed the drama of world events as they happened – fashions, television programmes, scandals – anything that would stave off the monotony of that particular kind of work that was so routine.

149

But one event was to repeat itself and the happy times came to an abrupt end when Emily angrily returned her work to the bench and walked out. Derek appeared to have become extremely irritated on a matter that concerned Geoffrey's work. He constantly niggled Emily with a barrage of criticism about her husband until she could take it no more. It was, in reality, a ploy that misfired. Times were hard again and there were rumbles of discontent from the bank as the sales of Minack produce took a tumble. Derek knew he had to cut back on the staff and he wrongfully thought that if he criticised Geoffrey Semmens to his wife, she in turn would sow the seed of discontent in her husband's mind and he would leave. The Tangyes could not afford any form of redundancy payment. Jeannie did not agree with Derek's tactics and she distanced herself. In the event it was Emily who left and Geoffrey who stayed. But a similar situation arose again in 1976, and then the two men parted company for the second time. But this time they were on better terms and they remained friends.

The second book of the *Minack Chronicles*, *A Cat At The Window*, was published in 1962. The following year, with a readership that was growing fast, Derek Tangye's third book, *A Drake At The Door*, was quickly chosen from the shelves of the leading bookshops. It was also a year for celebration as brother Nigel brought his bride, Moira, home to Glendorgal. Jeannie became very fond of her and the two women shared in good looks and personality. Moira brought a refreshing charm with her to Glendorgal and an even greater expertise than hitherto to enhance it as a summer hotel.

Derek remained jealous of the achievements of his brother, and also of many other authors who wrote books in a similar vein to his own. He became hostile in his feeling towards James Herriot – critical of his ability in writing the highly successful series of books *All Creatures Great And Small*. It was not until after Nigel had died that he allowed himself to become closer to Moira, whose support he valued when, just six months later, his brother Colin also died.

Moira discovered Derek was a man in constant need of reassurance. He often put himself down but did not take kindly to others who did it for him. More than one of his Copthorne School reports remarked that he had a need to feel liked and, as an adult, that sentiment had remained. His books became an extension of this need and when many of his readers trod the rough path to Dorminack to meet him, almost as a spiritual leader, he was deeply satisfied. Destiny, he discovered, had its envoys. The sales of his books were a yardstick by which to measure the affection of his readers. He had a need for them to feel they had come to understand him through his writing, in the same way they would understand their own fathers or brothers.

When two demure ladies visited him at Dorminack on one occasion, he discovered they had not purchased his current publication – a trilogy entitled *Great Minack Stories*. Their reason was that they already possessed the three volumes of the *Minack Chronicles* that were contained therein. He produced two copies and convinced them that, if they had been keen enough to meet him by walking the long and rough track to Dorminack, it would be a shame to return home without a memento. He signed each book and took their money without compunction.

Derek had a signing session in John Philpott's bookshop in Penzance. Up two flights of a wide stairway inside the elegant Camelot Court, other literary names rubbed shoulders on the bookshelves, almost as though they were eavesdropping on his conversations with his admiring readers. With some exceptions, many verbal exchanges amounted to nothing more than admirable chit-chat. It was an auspicious occasion with such a genial host and it was a successful one. At the end of the session, and when the customers had stopped arriving, Derek signed a further 18 copies of his current book for buyers who might arrive after he had left. He would not inscribe more, but gave instructions to John Philpott that if further readers wished for an autographed copy, they should make their way to Dorminack and meet him first.

151

Derek Tangye was married to a lady who was an expert in the skills of public relations and, through her, it was natural that he too should acquire such an ability. As a former journalist he also knew the value of photographs to illustrate a particular occasion. When the Cunard flagship, the *QE2*, sailed into Mount's Bay on a visit, the Captain was later to be received at Dorminack as an honoured guest. As the vessel passed Logan Rock it appeared, hugging the Minack coastline, and blasted a salute to Derek and Jeannie in its passing. Derek had already notified the press of the pre-arranged event and had also informed the tourist board. On that day even a helicopter hovered close by. Jeannie's sister Barbara and her husband Richard were on holiday and they were staying in Lamorna Cove. A makeshift flag was hoisted on the clifftop and as Derek and Jeannie posed holding Penny and Fred, two braying donkeys, they waved frantically and cheered loudly as the *QE2* slid majestically past Carne Barges.

Barbara was there but she had to remain an onlooker, not allowed to be any part of the action that occurred before the lens of the camera – an instrument which Derek had given to her husband Richard to operate. Click click click – the shutter snapped rapidly in the blinking of an eye and soon the First Lady of the Cunard Fleet had passed by and was navigating deeper waters. The feeling that the momentous occasion left in its wake at Minack was one of consuming elation. Derek took the camera from Richard to snap those present and to finish the film so that it could be processed. In the event, Derek could have been forgiven if he had thrown himself face down to the ground, in an image of desperation – for there was no film in the camera.

A photograph was, nevertheless, published in the *Minack Chronicles*; and it has remained a mystery to Barbara and Richard, Emily and Geoffrey Semmens and all others who were involved behind the camera on that day. The only answer to the mystery is the possibility of a contrived photo-shoot at a later date when the *QE2* made a return visit.

21

The purpose of this author is to present Derek Tangye and
Jean Nicol Tangye with a measure of understanding in the
continuity of their lives from the cradle to the grave – to try
to understand the strengths and weaknesses, the thoughts
and feelings that were not included in the *Minack Chronicles*. Derek and Jeannie's influence on others, the world
over, was immeasurable yet they were the first to consider
themselves humble mortals – but it had not always been
like that. When finally they both turned to a simple way of
life, many other people began to draw strength and hope
from what they did and the Minack meadows were suddenly
alive in people's minds as they read their words. As with all
beings and as children of an existence that remains a total
mystery in its purpose, Derek and Jeannie learned from
their mistakes in growing up and by the examples set to
them by others. Their interpretation was sometimes inaccur-
ate but it passed on an understanding of reason.

Minack is celebrated in the mind of whoever believes in the
chronicles. It is a dream that becomes a reality as the pages
are slowly turned. It is a place where problems may confront
the first light of each new day and by sundown all is well
once again and life has returned to near normal. There is a
manifestation of events that are gathered and stitched
together like the patches of a quilt that provides warmth for
all the admirers of the chronicles, as they escape their own
humdrum existence. The risk of a gamble can be shared
with the author because there is no reality of loss for the
reader.

Derek gave everything a name in Minack. Nothing was

153

without identity – whether it was a living creature or an inanimate object. One almost expected him to give a nickname to a marauding wind of gale force and to lovingly identify it once more should it return. Readers felt they knew the succession of cats who lived at Dorminack personally, whether they be Monty, Lama, Oliver, Ambrose or Cherry. There were the other beings also: the hen Queen Mary; the raucous seagulls the lager louts; the donkeys Merlin and Susie, Fred and Penny; not forgetting Boris the Muscovy duck – and many other creatures.

The meadows were related to their incidents or events, and were named accordingly. And visitors were keen to identify with them as such. 'Have we just crossed Monty's Leap?' 'Is that Carne Barges?' And when Derek tired of callers he would politely suggest they went and took a look at Oliver Land.

But the true enchantment in the legend of Minack is the love story – more real in writing than in actual life but, nevertheless, still bewitching by other people's standards. Many readers, the world over, compared the beautiful unshakeable romance in Derek and Jeannie's life in the clifftop meadows with the unsightly hair curlers and stale smells of their own marriages. With most of his readers being women, by the end of any one of his books, some of them actually fancied him. With Jeannie, it was her personality that contributed durably to her sex appeal.

Vic Gower, who started his working life at the Savoy Hotel as a 16-year-old, can remember today how he and all the other pageboys fell in love with her. To the reader, Derek and Jeannie became the perfect couple, bound in perfect love, and living together in perfect harmony. The fact was that this image gave so much happiness to so many people, in its acceptance, that Derek bent the maxim a little.

Of their love for each other, this author once suggested, 'The bond between you must have been very strong indeed to even contemplate living in what was a wilderness, knowing you would be on each other's backs for the rest of your lives – your love was surely charmed.'

154

This pleased Derek and he chuckled to himself as he replied, 'Yes, it's amazing when you look back on it – it sounds absolutely fantastic. But I don't know what it was. We had destiny – another thing – I think lots of people do have destiny – something inside them; it's not intellectual, its not even emotional – it's something that drives you forward. You feel you've got somewhere to go and, although I didn't write until I had the whole bloodstream feeling of what I was doing here, Jeannie wrote her book *Meet Me At The Savoy*, which was a fabulous book, and I didn't write until I felt I had got something to write about. Of course, as the chronicles have gone on, it's been one of the great pleasures, the fact I get lots of young people reading them – and they come here. The cottage is so difficult to find that people must be on one's wavelength, otherwise they wouldn't come.'

Derek was then asked, 'In many ways your books are about philosophy and I'm sure your readers have found them therapeutic. People today, by and large, have to live fast lives and many would dearly love to escape from it all – but risk is insecure. There must have been times, in the beginning, when you and Jeannie felt insecure.'

He was quick and most emphatic in his reply, 'Never – never, never – no, neither Jeannie or I ever doubted. I'll tell you what it is: life today is so glossy lots of people think everything has to be fed to them – we didn't feel that way. We felt there was something deeper in life that we had to put our hands into the soil – really suffer – to really get somewhere. Courage is, as I say, wrapped up in enthusiasm – because if you have enthusiasm you dare to approach courage – but you have dark moments – you have moments at three o'clock in the morning when you say "Christ almighty, how am I going to live?" We had moments in the past when we didn't have the money to pay for a postage stamp. We had times when we had lost all our crops. We were absolutely broke – but that didn't alter the fact we had enthusiasm – we both felt the same. The result of it all is the *Minack Chronicles* have been able to tell a real story. I

155

mean, it never has been, for instance, a phoney story – or a glossy story.'

All life within the Tangye domain became encapsulated and in his writing time was encouraged to stand still. Derek identified events in his life by the day or by the month in which they happened; never the year (that became classified information that could reveal to the reader the ages of both him and Jeannie). They both came to see themselves as being in an immortalised state, living in a Peter Pan land, and to identify something by giving it a complete date would be to initiate an ageing process. In his effort to hold time back, Derek would never allow Jeannie's sister Barbara to send her a birthday card even. When a writer of a magazine article gave his readers clues to Derek and Jeannie's ages Derek became angry, because he had led some of his close friends to believe he was a younger man. Vanity tucks itself away in all of us, more in some than in others. But in writing an autobiography – and he wrote his, in a sense, in 20 volumes – complete dates become important factors. Yet, unbelievably, his readers allowed him to get away with it. It seems that everyone who read the *Minack Chronicles* did so on his terms for, in doing so, they were offered an opportunity to become a Peter Pan also.

But the pen of Derek Tangye proved one thing very positively. Not everyone, in these times of terrible violence, wants to sit down and read literature that feeds the quirky facets of the mind with the sadistic stories that are designed to seize attention. One could almost refer to the Tangye books as "The Darling Buds of Minack" for all the happiness and pleasure they gave to others through his writing about their modest and seemingly untangled lifestyle. He knew the traits in the minds of the people he was writing for – and he assumed, quite rightly, they thought and felt like him. If they dipped in, everyone of them could find passages in his books they could identify with. Every woman knew by instinct that Jeannie was extremely feminine and that she possessed great strength – they could feel her zest for life. Her positive thoughts and her attitude were a mantle to others and this in turn encouraged many in overcoming their own problems.

There are countless potential Minacks throughout the British Isles – many still in Cornwall – there for those who feel, in some way, that they have a similar destiny in their veins. But if they meticulously pay their bills on time and are content to let the clock determine the events of their day, then they will already have a good idea of just what pattern is set for them for the rest of their lives – and they would be better just to read about the good life, for theirs is the life from which Derek and Jeannie had escaped. And, like them, they too will not move easily away from such an organised life; there has to be a big hand of dissatisfaction behind them, constantly pushing until they allow themselves to go with it. For those with the right temperament and commitment and, most important of all, those who also possess Derek and Jeannie's distinctive skills in writing; or have an ability to display another skill in the arts that can single them out with potential; there will always be others who will search them out in their devotion – the difficulty is in creating a carriage for such contact. As one Minack commits itself to the history of literature, there will always be room for another.

It will seem strange to some of his readers to learn that Derek Tangye was a very private man. His books were calculated to reveal only what he wanted others to know and, in painting such a picture, he chose his own colours. When he became a widower he sometimes interpreted himself as a bachelor and at such times he was much bolder in writing about the more intimate things in his life. He spent another ten years on his own – when some of the ladies who visited him became surrogate Jeannies. He even dared, through his own self-styled philosophy, to pay lip-service in his chronicles to the merits of open relationships in marriage.

Most times Jeannie walked in Derek's shadow as he wrote about their life together. Her own writing equalled the skill of his. But she had a second string to her bow –

her ability to write fiction, something he had attempted while still at Mortlake, and failed at. Later, at Minack, he stood on the high cliff at Carne Barges and tossed the manuscript into the sea in his frustration.

In 1965, Derek's *A Donkey In The Meadow* was published. *Lama* was about the wild black cat of the same name, who they named after the Dalai Lama, who was in the news at the time – it was published in 1966. In 1967, *Hotel Regina*, the first of Jeannie's hotel trilogies, was rejected by an agent, but the book was later to find its way onto reader's shelves and was to establish her as a writer of merit.

By now, readers the world over were becoming addicted to the *Minack Chronicles* and 1968 saw *The Way To Minack* published. This book gives a good account of their life before and at the beginning of Minack. *A Cornish Summer* made an appearance in 1970 and told of their animals and the pity they felt for the poor souls who failed to break free from their own environment. Two years later, in 1972, *Cottage On The Cliff* also came out and comfortably portrayed their contentment. It has to be said that each and every one of the *Minack Chronicles* is a jewel in its potential for the reader to discover their own contentment from deep within. In that same year, Derek's brother Nigel sold Glendorgal, thus ending a reign of ownership of generations of Tangyes. And from thereon it was the lodge house that became home for both him and his wife Moira and their young family.

In 1974, *A Cat Affair* was published. Jeannie produced *Home Is The Hotel* in 1976, and in 1978, there was Derek's *The Winding Lane*. *When The Winds Blow* was the thirteenth publication of the *Minack Chronicles*, in 1982; and in 1983, Jeannie's third and final story of the trilogy, *Bertioni's Hotel*, was as successful as the other two. In 1984 Derek published *A Quiet Year*, when he reflected on their continuing life at Minack.

22

Towards the end of 1985, Jeannie began to feel unwell. It was like her that she should not want anyone to know – not even Derek knew at first. It was not that she wished to make a secret of her feelings, but more that she did not want to be seen to be causing any unnecessary alarm. Just occasionally, in their life at Minack, both she and Derek had a twinge or a mild bout of sickness and found that, in refusing to accept its existence by talking about it, it eventually went away. But this time was different – a dull pain was stubborn in its refusal to go.

An appointment was made to see a specialist at a local hospital and she and Derek agreed that they would not tell close friends or relatives – not even when the problem had been put right. But, unknown to them, they were recognised waiting outside the consultant's examining room and this caused a mild flutter of speculation.

In September 1985, Jeannie was admitted to St Michael's Hospital in Hayle, Cornwall, an establishment that belonged to the Roman Catholic Order of the Daughters of the Cross of Liège. She had cancer of the bowel and immediately underwent four hours of surgery. The operation was considered, at first, to be successful and in time she was discharged. Derek had explained her absence by saying she had gone to Derbyshire to stay with her sister Barbara. Now, they thought, they could get on with their lives and there was no reason why anyone should need to know of the illness. Even in her darkest moments, prior to the operation, Jeannie led the way once more by showing a much greater strength than her husband possessed. And it was that strength, and the elation at having survived the cancer, that gave her and Derek a few more months of happiness that surpassed any they had experienced hitherto. Their perception of life was enhanced spiritually and with an even deeper meaning than before. A check-up and an X-ray in November confirmed that all was well and Christmas that year was, once again, enjoyed by Jeannie in childlike wonderment.

But things did *not* go right and the pain returned. Jeannie was readmitted to St Michael's Hospital at the end of January 1986. She underwent further surgery and it was known then that she had terminal cancer.

She was in room 207 (symbolically just two doors down the corridor from room 205, the number of her publicity office at the Savoy Hotel). It took on the enchantment of one of the rooms of the "Alice's palace" of her childhood imagination as Derek decorated it with the jackets of each book both he and she had written. He visited her twice a day and each morning he brought fresh flowers that had grown in the soil she had happily laboured in at Minack. Still no one else, outside the hospital, knew that her life was slipping gently away and, as a result, she had no visitors other than Derek – such was her wish and he felt at her command.

Jeannie remained very feminine, even at the end, and before each of Derek's visits she took care with her cosmetics. Her jewellery box was beside her bed and she took great care as she picked each piece over and fondly related it to its particular memory. As she held a necklace to her, she became a princess who waited patiently for her prince to call. As partners, they had sailed rough waters in the early part of their marriage, before each had discovered how to handle the other's helm. More stable in her emotions than he was in his, she had soon learned to tolerate his idiosyncrasies.

Now, as she grew weaker, she lay quietly in her hospital bed with vivid recollections of her past life: quarter past twelve in the little chapel that was part of Richmond church when, wearing a bridal gown that had been exclusively created for her by Norman Hartnell, she joined Derek at the altar. She remembered the warm smile of Colin, who was about to become her brother-in-law, as he stood looking regal in his role as the groom's best man. There was such a long journey to go through in her memory – and she wanted to remember it all, yet she knew she had so little time in which to do it. The dim light that shone in her hospital room at night became, in her mind's eye, the moonlight over the meadows of Minack once again – it was midnight on Good Friday and she was standing beside Derek, with Monty the ginger cat in her arms; they had just arrived. They were young and they were bursting with enthusiasm and energy. There was a lot to do and a lifetime ahead of them in which to do it. The meadows were overgrown with weeds that constantly produced strange flowers of happiness. Silvered beams of moonlight gave a surreal lustre to the weather-worn granite of Carne Barges. The calm water of Mount's Bay glittered from the opened bedroom window at Dorminack. Home was now a patched-up cottage with no water on tap and a primitive form of sanitation. Paraffin gave them light and warmth and it also cooked their food. Their adventure had just begun.

With a fabric of life that was in utter contrast to that of the big city, they now depended only on themselves. If the lights went out all over the land – and they did through industrial unrest – then it mattered not. Destiny was *walking* with them now instead of preceding them – and it kept pace. Jeannie remembered how happily they had anticipated that future and, in reality, how different were so many of the events that occurred.

Nursing Sister Margaret Davies was one of those who lovingly tended and cared for Jeannie, and the two women instantly became very firm friends. Like Jeannie, Sister Davies possessed a positive personality and a strong character. They recognised in each other the same will and its strength – and each regarded the other with a deep spiritual respect. With a mutual love of cats, they sealed their nurse–patient relationship. Sister Davies took Porker, one of her own cats, to the hospital for a meeting with Jeannie. He

161

purred and bumped Jeannie's hand with his head and the meeting was an instant success. As therapy, Porker's ability to lift Jeannie's heart was instantly effective. In her appreciation, Jeannie presented Sister Margaret with a copy of her book *Meet Me At The Savoy* and in it she wrote: 'To Margaret, with so many thanks for all your care and kindness. Best Wishes. Jean Nicol Tangye.'

On Monday, 10 February 1986, Derek was spoken to once again by the surgeon, who advised him of what was now inevitable – and close. Jeannie was admired by everyone, from those with the most menial of tasks in the hospital, to the most highly skilled. She had accepted, with the utmost of courage, that she was dying and she asked Sister Davies to be there with her at the end. She continued to smile and she thanked those who tried to make her comfortable. As her body grew weaker her inner resolve remained strong. She was an inspiration to all who nursed her – and as one simple and mortal soul she made them all feel proud of their profession and everything it had ever stood for.

Derek signed a copy of his book *A Gull On The Roof* and presented it to Sister Davies' parents for the occasion of their golden wedding anniversary. After visiting Jeannie on the eve of that particular February day, he parked his car on the seafront in Penzance and walked to the premier Queens Hotel – a place he and Jeannie sometimes used as a local substitute for the Savoy.

In his loneliness, he remained outside like a hungry waif, almost pressing his face against the window of the restaurant. He saw the happiness of the honoured couple as they joined their guests at the anniversary celebration. He knew he would have been welcomed inside had he made an appearance – but he had just left his wife in a hospital bed where she was losing her fight for life. He prayed that Jeannie would be able to hold on just long enough that they would be able mark the forty-third anniversary of their own wedding day. They had passed their ruby – but sadly there would be no gold for him and Jeannie.

Jean Nicol Tangye died early on Saturday morning, 22 February 1986. She had waited for Sister Margaret Davies to come on duty. It was just two days after her wedding anniversary, when she and Derek had started their forty-fourth year together. Another four weeks and it would have been her birthday – she would have been 67 years of age, and still so young.

No one was more qualified to join the spirits of Minack than Jean Nicol Tangye and, in doing so, she realised the infinity of her own prose: where life continues and death is never. In that short statement, the legend of Jeannie has breathed life into the granite that supports the clifftop meadows and will continue to do so until they crumble into the sea.

There was still no telephone installed at Dorminack, so Sister Margaret Davies had to wait until after 8 am for Derek to make a call from his usual box in the hamlet of Sheffield. He took the news calmly. Afterwards, he telephoned Barbara at her home in Derbyshire who, intuitively, already knew of her sister's death. Then he returned to the cottage at Minack to be alone in his sorrow and his tears. He had never come to terms with Jeannie's illness – so what hope was there for him now in her death? He did not see her body laid out for he wished to remember her as he had known her in life. But those who tended her after her passing dressed her in an attractive Victorian lace nightdress and observed that the lines had miraculously left her face – making her look as much as 30 years younger.

Sister Davies stated, 'You couldn't help loving her. Jeannie was a most remarkable lady – one of the most unforgettable I have met in my life. I have been in the nursing profession for over forty years and it was indeed a privilege to have nursed someone like her. There was always a closeness between nurse and patient.'

Jean Nicol Tangye was cremated at Truro, nearly an hour's drive from Minack. The crematorium was packed with relatives and friends, many of whom had travelled great distances, who wished to show their respect in worship

163

for her. Her sister Barbara stayed the previous night with her husband Richard at the Lamorna Hotel, and on the morning of the funeral they drove the rough track to Dorminack to collect Derek. He was not ready and claimed he had to 'hoover' the living room and the bedroom. He was finding that all conversation, no matter how caring, was still intrusive. Barbara and Richard were not invited into the cottage and they patiently sat in their car, on an extremely cold morning, until he was finished.

He was an individualist once more – he was melancholy and wished only for his own company. But Barbara and Richard were finally invited into the cottage for a drink with him, before he màde that final journey to commit his wife's memory to all who loved her. It was to be an uncomfortable day for him – obligated, in his sadness, to smile and shake hands with the assembly of people who had gathered at Truro. He decided, at the last minute, to drive on his own to the crematorium, and afterwards he returned to the isolated cottage where he had once lived, brimming with happiness, with a wife who, he was convinced, was more beautiful and more exciting than any other woman on earth. His friend, writer David Cornwell, lived just a short distance across the meadows in another isolated cottage and had kindly offered to provide close mourners with refreshments.

Jeannie's ashes were scattered in a clifftop meadow at Minack – and so her greatest wish of all was achieved. With her passing, Derek had lost some of his spiritual strength but was still encouraged through *her* inspiration. For 43 years he had been blessed with the good fortune of having an exceptional woman in his life, the like of whom he would never experience again. Jeannie was not a freak – for there were others like her in the world – but Derek knew it would not be possible for him to find another woman whose imprint of mind would match his in quite the same way. But – and it was a very doubtful but – in moments when his loneliness stole the lucidity of his mind, he sometimes felt there might be a second-best partner who would appear to him, like a deity of his imagination, as she trod the uneven path that crossed Monty's Leap and knocked on the cottage door.

To be an individualist is sometimes to be derided as a loner, but to be a loner is not to be *immune* to the pain of loneliness. Suddenly, others saw the cottage of Dorminack without Jeannie as a vessel that was half empty – but, in actual fact, with Derek continuing to live there it was half full, an interpretation he readily agreed with. The couple had made a pact in their early days of settlement at Minack that whoever should depart first the other would remain.

For Derek, his adult life before Jeannie had few memories that left him with any deep satisfaction. It was she who gave him the strength and hope that he had carried forward from the start of their relationship. Until he met her he had many false starts in life that also demanded false values of him – with which he had never really reconciled himself. And then the consequence of arrogance and intolerance burdened him with two Achilles heels. From the beginning Jeannie had rapped his knuckles when there had been a need and she had been an example to him by not responding to his prejudices.

For ten years, after Jeannie's death, Derek was the wizard of Minack at the end of a long granite track. And just by meeting those who had braved the hazards of that long trek, he gave many admirers a strength to lift a burden from their own path or to cope with an illness – some even claimed to have been cured when conventional medicine had failed them. He inspired confidence in others, when he had continuously suffered a lifetime's feeling of insecurity himself. When writing or talking to readers about the *Minack Chronicles* he possessed the power of influence over many of them.

He had never forgotten those early days at Minack when he and Jeannie were financially broken and plagued by demands for payment of debts – at that time they both would have welcomed a postal strike to give them a little respite. Each day the postman's red van impelled its way down the better part of the track to leave the Tangye post at a nearby farmhouse. Among the letters there would sometimes be one that was intimidating, and written by a despotic hand of a creditor. In the hard-up days, the Tangyes had kept hens that produced far more eggs than they needed for themselves. They sold the extras to a middleman who got around in an old vehicle that could only manage the track as far as the farm – beyond that the way ahead became known as an exhaust pipe cruncher. A neighbour, in a cottage close to the farm, kindly allowed the eggs to be left there for the man's collection. It was a time when country people could safely leave their homes unoccupied and with the windows opened wide. On one occasion the neighbour had gone to shop in town leaving the egg money in its usual place in the kitchen. The Tangyes were so pushed for every penny that it was spent before it was earned. Jeannie called at the cottage, keen for the egg takings, only to discover the neighbour's absence. In an act of desperation, she climbed through an opened downstairs window and collected the money – such was their dilemma.

Jane worked at Minack in her teenage years. When she started, Derek and Jeannie needed the help to boost production; but they could afford to pay her very little in wages. Colleagues were unaware of the Tangye financial crisis and they kidded Derek that Jane did not really need to earn generous wages as she had an inheritance that was more than sufficient for her needs. Such was a charade of naive deception that Jane, in her innocence, had to accept but did not enter into. But with thoughts of insecurity of tenure at Minack on his mind, Derek took the story seriously and had a quiet word with Jane. He asked her for a loan, and was as embarrassed as she was when she had to disclose the well meaning hoax to him.

23

Living on his own and growing older, Derek Tangye managed to survive in his ability to write – although he continued with a tendency to repeat himself. Ever popular, as an author, his readers remained eager to dip into the pages as each new volume of the *Minack Chronicles* was published. Jeannie had typed the manuscript of *The Cherry Tree*, completing it after returning home and convalescing from her major operation for cancer in St Michael's Hospital. It was sent to the publisher before she was readmitted to that hospital and it appeared in the bookshops that same year, 1986, but after she had died.

Two years later, 1988 saw the appearance of Derek's love story *Jeannie*, in which he relived the dying moments of his wife's life. Some hold this to be his best writing. In it he recalls much of their life together and parts are passionately deep and moving. If readers are overcome with such emotion themselves, then they would be merely crying along with him as he lovingly chose each word that he wrote.

The Evening Gull was published in 1990, in which he talks about life on his own and he takes the occasional stroll backwards through the leafy lanes of his life. As time went by, he was convinced that Jeannie was spiritually there with him. He sometimes told Tracy, a young mother who was the daughter-in-law of a far neighbour and who had become his domestic helper, that Jeannie often appeared in the cottage and it comforted him. He would often insist that Tracy have a glass of wine with him before she started her daily chores and, on one occasion, he told her that Jeannie was standing behind her – also holding a glass of wine. He truly believed that he perceived her spiritually and that it would be cruel for any non-believers to scoff at his claims,

167

because they too would be gratified and privileged to see, once again, someone who had departed from their life – someone whom they held the closest in their heart.

Monty's Leap was published in 1993 and, although it was another edition of the *Minack Chronicles* and welcomed by his readers, it essentially mirrored much of what he had already written about. The title came from that momentous leap that Monty the cat, who arrived with them from London, had taken over the tiny stream that forded the path that led to the cottage door on that moonlit Good Friday night in 1950 – when they had first become domiciled at Minack. In using the caption once more and so long after the event he had, in a sense, brought their life in the Cornish clifftop meadows full circle – at a time when the first few grains of the sand that would mark the end of his own life had already begun to fall to the bottom of the glass.

It was natural that each volume of the *Minack Chronicles* he had written and published since Jeannie's death should also, by and large, rejoice in her life and revive his fond memories of her. But he was once again talking more freely – more about harmless flirtations, and open marriages were being spoken of. His philosophy had opened up somewhat, like the petals of a flower whose face still needed the warmth of the sun. He had never been a man who took on board new ideas readily, so the reader of his final book *The Confusion Room* is led to believe that the words and feelings that he expressed therein had been tucked away, for much of his life, in a distant recess of the mind.

The aptly named Confusion Room was, in actual fact, at the far end of an outbuilding that was the stable where the donkeys were sometimes kept; and it was in close proximity to the cottage. But the room was also designated for human habitation, and Derek and Jeannie had used it as such, to sleep in when there was a need that they should vacate their own bedroom to accommodate a distinguished guest.

Lovable and often the worse for his slight state of inebriation, George Brown was Foreign Secretary in Harold Wilson's Labour Government in the 1960s. Politically, he was a controversial figure and when he resigned his cabinet post he decided to lie low – for he knew that those who mustered the news media would stalk him like big game hunters. Having notified Derek and Jeannie of his decision to hide away at Dorminack (not *ask* for sanctuary), he arrived under the cover of darkness with his wife and they were given possession of the tiny master bedroom in the cottage. Derek, as a younger man and a supporter to the right of all political philosophy, had learned to acquire an attitude of neutrality on Fleet Street. But a difference in opinion with someone so entrenched in contemporary socialist dogma as George Brown was irritating to him – especially when theories of other controversial figures were thrown at him as a challenge. He found himself obliged to listen to words that talked of a pattern of social organisation that reflected the very same structure as the life that he and Jeannie had escaped from – only now it was being spoken of as though it was a new political concept in the nation's way forward.

As a political campaigner George Brown never kissed babies: instead, his vulnerability made the mums want to kiss him. And the irony was that George Brown and his wife were at Minack for a reason that ran parallel with that of the Tangyes – to escape, and to redeem the freedom of their minds by using the embrocation of the very same Cornish clifftop meadows.

Other uses for the Confusion Room were as a writing studio, workshop, a place of convenience. Now it served as a storeroom also, and it encapsulated the whole of Derek's life. The contents were stored without orchestration or arrangement – which is how much of his life could be viewed before, of course, Jeannie had inspired him in its purpose. There was memorabilia, much of which acted as signposts in retracing his footsteps. The room was a repre-sentation of his mind in that it contained his memory and it revealed aspects of his personality. There were recollections of happy experiences among the mementos and of a few encounters he would rather forget. Cardboard boxes on the

169

wooden shelves contained his ego in the countless letters of admiration he had received over the years that spanned the collective life of all the *Minack Chronicles*. His diaries were there too – as fingerprints of his experiences. They were documents he had already mentioned in the chronicles as being passages of the mind and only he knew the code that would unlock their precise interpretation. The first requirement of any reader who would attempt such a task would be the need to possess the mind of an individualist to first define Derek's own understanding of himself – an understanding that he had sometimes subconsciously camouflaged in that daily log of occurrences.

The room was, in fact, two minds merged into one – for Jeannie was there also, her memory, her talents, her personality. She was now the silent partner; yet *she* had been his strength – without her, Derek's Confusion Room may well have been in a shed in the back garden of a rented suburban semi-detached house somewhere in Surrey.

It has been said that many people sense an approaching end to their life; and when they do they make the effort to put their affairs in order. Derek Tangye was not the most orderly of people yet he found himself, on his knees, sifting through his life. The evidence of what he left behind would be used by others to become a part of his character for posterity. He was a very private man – although his writing *had* been essentially autobiographical. He was private, in that he wrote of himself on his own terms. In terms of psychology, the id is to the unconscious mind what the ego is to the conscious mind – Derek's id was his custodian and his mental editor, his ego was his status in being celebrated by others.

Over the many years that he and Jeannie had been at Minack, readers had constantly visited them. And since Jeannie's death Derek had sat in the conservatory at Dorminack and received his visitors daily. After a period of discussion he would politely walk with them along the path at the side of the cottage to see them off: which was so often when he had tired of their company. Many of those

admirers came time and time again and eventually interpreted themselves as being a friend of some value to him.
He placed no real value on any of them in a personal sense
and he could count those whom he had chosen to be close
to him in little more than the number of keys on the
QWERTY row of his typewriter. To be accepted as a true
friend of his was to become a member of an exclusive
fellowship.

Derek Tangye's most cherished memories were, in all
reality, retrospective only to his first glimpse of Jeannie.
When he reached 80 years of age, the recollections of much
of his young bachelor life had faded into a recall that was
surreal. To be young is to have very little past life, but the
promise of a future that looks bountiful and constant in a
passage of time that seemingly stretches to infinity – to be
old is to have one hand already outstretched in anticipation
of opening the final door that will *lead* to that infinity. Age
reinterprets the values of youth.

Canon Andrews was a relative of Jeannie's and at the
age of 100 years he was still living on his own and coping. It
was Derek's determination that he would do the same. But
he was aware that such a resolve to stay put *could* shorten
his life also; for should he be stricken with a persistent
illness he would refuse hospitalisation and remain
entrenched at Dorminack until his dying day. He had no
control over his coming into this world, but he would leave
it on his own terms.

In October 1995, Cherry, the last of the Minack cats,
became ill and died. The nights became lonely for Derek
now and, for the very first time, there was no companion to
share his bed with. Jeannie had discovered Cherry under
the cherry tree close to the cottage and, after her own
passing, the cat had helped to fill a chasm in Derek's heart.
Now that gap had opened once more.

Now more frail than ever before, Derek was very fortunate, for a platoon of friends watched him constantly and
took care of his needs. He drank a little more, sometimes
asking a known caller to get a bottle of vodka from the

171

supply that he kept stowed in the boot of his car. It was so long since Jeannie had died and still so many of the people who trekked to Minack had not heard of the event and, as time passed, it remained difficult to conceal the emotional strain. There were ladies who stayed in the cottage with him; but they were merely close friends and, as consorts, were there to comfort him and not to usurp the love that Jeannie had left in his care like a priceless gemstone.

Derek Alan Trevithick Tangye died on 26 October 1996, in the tiny bedroom of the cottage that looked out over Monty's Leap towards Oliver Land. It was a Saturday – the same day of the week on which his beloved wife Jeannie had departed just over ten years earlier. His heart had failed him.

Yet another event at Minack was to go full circle; for Harold Thomas was the undertaker who conveyed him, with dignity, to prepare him for his cremation. Harold, together with his father, Ashley Thomas, had helped to establish Derek and Jeannie at Dorminack 46 years earlier by building a new roof – a roof that was paid for by instalments that were determined by just how much the Tangyes felt they could afford at the time. Harold had helped Derek into Minack and now he would take him on a final journey that would place him beyond all he had ever felt, as a younger man, was the ultimate in his destiny. The cottage of Dorminack had completed yet another chapter in its existence on a Cornish clifftop – a chapter that time had already started to process as an addendum to its history.

24

This chapter is intended to be one of celebration for those who discovered the lives of Derek and Jeannie Tangye. Their memory has become a celebration of encapsulated time that remains stable on a planet that continues to leap forward, unnecessarily fast, in a progressive evolution that possesses an unbelievable power to destroy itself in so many ways, where each new generation witnesses the seed of greed and many acts of inhumane savagery somewhere on earth.

Each one of Derek Tangye's books can be a waterhole to satisfy a thirst in an oasis of the mind – an added dimension to the inner eye, a meaningful statement that was born of frustration with the life that existed, for him and for her, on a planet which sometimes distressed them and sometimes excited them – and a place from which we are all frightened to be parted.

The reader of modern fiction, on the other hand, is all too often lost in a make-believe world, aroused by the terrible violence that besieges us in our normal day-to-day existence, where every story must have at least one body, an involvement of pain and suffering, and explicit detail of gore. The average make-believe story readers *fear* the very violence they demand in their reading and viewing; and a fortune in public funding is spent each year to prevent the type of crimes that stimulate their minds in literature.

When Derek and Jeannie Tangye died they became bonded as spiritual partners. Peace and contentment settled comfortably over Minack and the remnants of the physical lives they left behind were scattered over the new growth that had begun to sprout in Honeysuckle Meadow. Before the relatives and friends, who had attended both ceremonies, had gone home the gentle wind had carried particles of their ashes, in the same manner that it conveyed seeds, to settle sympathetically on the other meadows of the clifftop. This ensured that Derek and Jeannie were merged with the soil they had lovingly toiled in – which means they will continue to be a physical part of all that will ever grow in the loam of Minack. Every flower, every herb, every tree, every shrub, every weed, will be a representation of the spirit of their lives through endless biological evolution.

Those are not symbolically romantic words; they are, in fact, a statement in actuality. For, as the molecular structure of their ashes quite naturally broke down under natural laws that have existed since the beginning of the phenomenon of light and dark, the atoms contained therein were quite naturally redistributed and became part of other molecules: as a resource they will assist the meadows to flourish for a time that is beyond human comprehension. Spiritually, one only has to visit Oliver Land to be curiously aware of their eternal survival there – and the feeling of a friendly hand laid gently on one's shoulder.

If the power of rational thinking and of memory were to suddenly fail, the human race would have to survive on instinct alone and it is very probable all forms of higher intelligent life would decline. But this is exactly how Derek and Jeannie Tangye were able to motivate themselves in 1950 – by challenging the principles of other people's so-called sound judgement and having a willingness to put behind them, for a while at least, the memories of a previous way of life in London: a way that offered them a degree of comfort and a pattern of security – albeit questionable to them at the time. They became pioneers in an already settled land, where, each day, the poorer quality of living they were prepared to accept was commensurate with walking back 100 years or so, into a way of life that would have quite naturally existed at Minack: a time when Derek's great-grandfather, Joseph Tangye, attended the Friends Meeting House in Redruth, Cornwall, as a dedicated Quaker.

174

Self-sufficiency will always provide a feeling of independence for anyone who seeks and gains it, but usually only after taking that first and, sometimes almost impossible, fortuitous one league step of the mind.

For 18 months after Derek's passing, the cottage of Dorminack remained empty. The clifftop meadows had become less productive as he had grown older but, to each visitor, his continued presence there eclipsed the vision of decay and rugged repossession by nature that was then evident. Jeannie had left him as the keeper of Minack – and, given his circumstances, he had not let her down.

Today, the Register of Buildings of Architectural and Historic Interest held by English Heritage lists the cottage of Dorminack and the stable (that incorporates the Confusion Room at one end) as being Grade II. Derek set up the Minack Chronicles Trust before he died and each Trustee he appointed was a valued and trusted friend. The main purpose of the Trust is to further the published works of both him and his wife Jeannie and to preserve the nature reserve that is known as Oliver Land where the legendary donkeys once roamed freely. It was anticipated very early on that this "place of solitude" would one day become a haven where those with negatives ergs of the mind might sit quietly and meditate in an attempt to feel the scattered seeds of nature enter their heart and their soul. Jeannie was the first to discover such a subsistence in the tranquillity that dwelled in the meadow when she began to use Carne Barges as a place of private worship – where she felt warmed in the company of the spirits of Minack.

In the months that followed Derek's passing there were numerous applications to the office of Lord Falmouth's Estate for the tenancy of the vacant cottage known as Dorminack, by then hushed and encroached upon by nature's overgrowing tendrils. Each entrant was genuine in his or her desire to live in the Cornish clifftop outpost. The fortunate candidates were Jane Bird and her partner Peter Clough with their seven-year-old border collie, Twig. They took over in March 1998.

Jane had worked for Derek and Jeannie Tangye as a teenage girl and had moved on in a journey of exploration, with a heartfelt need for greater knowledge and for hands-on experience, in the field of horticulture. Today she is an expert in her calling. Peter, in his time, has given talks to audiences of enthusiasts in many parts of the country, has been listened to on radio and watched on television. He too is an expert. Together, their specialities are ferns, irises and plants that grow in coastal climatic conditions, which they will be selling wholesale and by retail mail order. But the first of many of their big tasks was to start clearing the clifftop meadows of a decade of encroaching brambles and scrub. Gradually, and in time, Minack will return to something of the order that Jane remembers when, once, she walked to work each morning along the path from her home perched close by on the clifftop.

The legend of Nicol-Tangye's Minack is a buttress that helps to shore up the traditional beliefs in unpretentious folklore – and it was built on a cornerstone that supported a love story that was envied by others. Like all human beings, Derek and Jeannie were not perfect people – which is a thankful deliverance, because the flawless mind is somehow unreal, incomplete and uninteresting. They took pleasure in an ability to dream with their eyes open – and such was their doctrine that it bolstered their minds to ultimately prevail over all that was evil in the world. The clifftop meadows became a sanctuary for every living creature that wished to share with them.

People are varied in their personalities and most have an element of creativity in their minds. If 12 individualists inhabit the same space, then there will be a dozen different pictures painted – or 12 different stories written – because such people must be allowed the freedom of their own expression in order to flourish. But if that same space is occupied by human beings who prefer to cooperate with each other as teamsters, then that crew will work comfortably together in the creation of an end product. The individualist feels claustrophobic in the symbolic world of the assembly line and mass production techniques. And so, in the packing sheds of Minack where the work was so often repetitious, there was always a sense of harmony as Jeannie encouraged separate minds in personalised thinking and choice.

In the pre-Minack days, Thames Bank Cottage in Mortlake was significant as a halfway house and a turning point for Derek in his introspective search for meaning in his life. For Jeannie it was a mere staging post – she had always had ambition and a good idea of where she was going. They possessed different personality traits yet they were both individualists.

It became commonplace, in those immediate post-war days, for minds to look for a better life when countless ex-servicemen were unsure of job security in the civilian life that was on offer to them. So many took their families to a new life in Canada, Australia, or New Zealand – and many of those emigrants were Cornish. Derek and Jeannie Tangye settled in the land they left behind – mother Cornwall, a place they loved more than any other in the world.

If Marie Curie had not lived it was inevitable that, in time, someone else would have discovered radium. If Albert Einstein had not been around, a like mind would have eventually considered his theory of relativity. Both people were individualists and, as such, they were dedicated to their cause and gave a precious gift to humanity. But if Derek and Jeannie Tangye had not lived, or even met, it can be positively said, there would be no *Minack Chronicles* in the archives today and there would not exist a nature reserve Trust with which to protect the ring of precious stone that mother Cornwall now wears proudly on her finger.

Today the cottage of Dorminack is wired for electricity and plumbed for bottled gas. There is fresh water on tap, automatically pumped from a well that was drilled and blasted 30 feet into the granite rock; this has also enabled the installation of modern sanitation. Even a telephone is heard to ring. One hundred years from now, once again, some of those living conventions will probably be considered to be primitive by the enhanced standards of the day. There will surely continue to be a little robin who hops around in friendly curiosity and perches on the wooden gate beside the stable – and an evening gull to be seen resting on the chimney. Those creatures will always be just a small part of the folklore of Minack.

Chapter one of this book is about Derek Tangye. In that sense he has had the first word; so it is fair that the very last comment should come from his wife: Jean Nicol Tangye. And it is to quote from the very last page of her book, *Meet Me At The Savoy*, which she wrote at Minack after she resigned from her busy life as the head of public relations for the Savoy Hotel Group:

> ... A year has passed and I am sitting in our two-roomed cottage, perched snugly above the Cornish sea, dreaming back over the years. There is no sound except the call of the gulls and the contented purring of Monty who is curled on my knee. The sunlight floods in through the open door, bringing with it the mingled fragrance of gorse and violets. The bright china glows on the dresser and the smell of baking from the oven warns me that my apple-pie is ready. I think, without regret, of the backless evening-dresses, the satin cocktail suits, the champagne and the flattery, when Derek calls to me from the garden.
>
> 'Darling, I'm just filling in the census and it's really rather embarrassing. At the bottom they put, "Have you a bathroom? Have you a kitchen sink? Have you a lavatory? Have you running water?" and I've had to put "No" to the whole lot.'
>
> I laughed and hugged Monty. I would not live anywhere else in the world, I thought, as I went to rescue the apple-pie.

POSTSCRIPT

This book has been written in the memory of Derek and Jeannie Tangye and the author hopes that it will assist in keeping the *Minack Chronicles* vibrantly alive in the minds of their readers and be an introduction to those who are yet to discover them.

As absorbing literature, the chronicles can be read time and again or simply dipped into in quiet moments and, as such, the books are well worth keeping within reach on the bookshelves of every home – for there are few people who would not identify with them in some way.

For the devotee of Tangye's Minack, there is information available on continuing events in the Cornish clifftop meadows and this can be read in the *Minack News*. This is in the form of a news sheet that has a large mailing list and is published regularly by Anne and Malcolm Sutton, The Old Sunday School, Carfury, Newmill, Penzance, Cornwall, TR20 8XZ.